Oxford First
Illustrated
Dictionary

OXFORD
UNIVERSITY PRESS

OXFORD
UNIVERSITY PRESS

Great Clarendon Street, Oxford OX2 6DP

Oxford University Press is a department of the University of Oxford.
It furthers the University's objective of excellence in research, scholarship,
and education by publishing worldwide in

Oxford   New York

Auckland   Cape Town   Dar es Salaam   Hong Kong   Karachi
Kuala Lumpur   Madrid   Melbourne   Mexico City   Nairobi
New Delhi   Shanghai   Taipei   Toronto

With offices in

Argentina   Austria   Brazil   Chile   Czech Republic   France   Greece
Guatemala   Hungary   Italy   Japan   Poland   Portugal   Singapore
South Korea   Switzerland   Thailand   Turkey   Ukraine   Vietnam

Oxford is a registered trade mark of Oxford University Press
in the UK and in certain other countries

British Library Cataloguing in Publication Data

Data available

ISBN-13: 978-0-19-910913-5 hardback
ISBN-10: 0-19-910913-3 hardback

ISBN-13: 978-0-19-838573-8 paperback
ISBN-10: 0-19-838573-0 paperback

1 3 5 7 9 10 8 6 4 2

Printed by KHL Printing Co. Pte Ltd

Oxford First
Illustrated
Dictionary

Compiled by
Andrew Delahunty

Illustrated by
Emma Chichester Clark

OXFORD
UNIVERSITY PRESS

Introduction

This dictionary is a first dictionary
that children, parents, and teachers will love.

◆ 2000 dictionary entries in alphabetical order

It introduces young children to the idea of a dictionary and helps them develop early dictionary skills.

It is authoritative in the information it gives on spelling, meaning, and usage, and it also creates a sense of magic that draws the reader into the empowering world of language and learning.

Every page invites the reader to think about words in an active way. All the headwords have been carefully selected to match children's current reading, writing, and speaking habits. Definitions are clear and simple, always given in full sentences, and use vocabulary a younger reader will be familiar with.

Examples show how the words are used and explain their meaning further through favourite children's story characters from Aladdin to Winnie-the-Pooh, Cinderella to Rumpelstiltskin.

◆ clear and simple meanings given in full sentences

◆ synonyms and opposites

◆ spelling and pronunciation and word building help

◆ hundreds of examples taken from well-known nursery rhymes, fairy tales, and songs

 ◆ rhyming words

 ◆ idioms

◆ word origins

The humour and snippets of word-based information will appeal to a wide audience. A huge array of language information is packed in: rhyming words, synonyms and antonyms, the origins of words, alongside features not usually found in dictionaries such as hundreds of language jokes, riddles, puns, and anagrams.

This wealth of material encourages readers to roam around the dictionary picking up essential reference and language skills along the way.

Emma Chichester Clark's illustrations appear on every page. Six characters appear throughout and play important roles. The pictures are imaginative and playful compositions that often incorporate a number of different words in the same scene. Young readers will soon be drawn in to the dictionary by spotting which words are illustrated.

We hope children enjoy exploring language with this dictionary. Language is a powerful tool in life, and we hope that this dictionary will help provide readers with the first and essential literacy skills to equip them for the future.

The author, illustrator, and publishers are most grateful to all those teachers whose comments and suggestions have helped shape this book and make it as useful as possible to all primary school children.

◆ riddles, tips, and lots of amazing language facts

◆ special thematic picture section at the end

How to use the dictionary

What is a dictionary for? A dictionary tells you what a word means and how to spell it. The words in a dictionary are listed in alphabetical order.

Headwords
The blue words on each page are called headwords. These are the words that are explained in the dictionary. The headwords are arranged in alphabetical order.

Extra information
Examples of the headword in an alphabetical list

Word classes
(Parts of speech) The word class tells you what job the headword does when it's used in a sentence. For example, you can see if the headword is a noun, a verb, or an adjective.

Definitions
A definition tells you what the word means. Some words in the dictionary have more than one meaning and so more than one definition.

Extra information
Language and word building information

---

fish – flash

a b c d e **f** g h i j k l m n o p q r s t u v w x y z

fish *noun* (fish or fishes)
A fish is an animal that lives and breathes under water. Fish are covered with scales, and they have fins and a tail for swimming.
◆ There are many different types of fish. Here are some of them: carp, cod, eel, goldfish, haddock, halibut, herring, mackerel, perch, pike, pilchard, plaice, salmon, sardine, seahorse, shark, sole, trout.

fish *verb* (fishes, fishing, fished)
If you fish, you try to catch fish.

fit *verb* (fits, fitting, fitted)
If something fits you, it is the right size and shape.
The glass slipper fitted Cinderella perfectly.

fit *adjective* (fitter, fittest)
Someone who is fit is healthy.

five *noun* (fives)
Five is the number 5.
◆ In this dictionary, the word that comes after five is not six but . . . fix!
Some other words that end with the letters 'ive' are: alive dive drive hive

fix *verb* (fixes, fixing, fixed)
1 If you fix something that is broken, you mend it.
Can you fix my computer?
2 If you fix something somewhere, you join it firmly to something else.

fizzy *adjective* (fizzier, fizziest)
A fizzy drink is one that is full of little bubbles. If a drink fizzes, it makes a hissing sound because of all the little bubbles.
◆ Some words sound like the thing they mean. The word fizzy actually sounds like the hissing sound that the bubbles make in a fizzy drink.

flag *noun* (flags)
A flag is a piece of cloth with a pattern on it. It is used as a symbol of a country or a group of people.

flame *noun* (flames)
A flame is one of the hot, bright strips of light you see rising up from a fire.
◆ Some other words that end with the letters 'ame' are: blame frame game name same tame

flap *verb* (flaps, flapping, flapped)
When a bird flaps its wings, it moves them up and down quickly.

flash *noun* (flashes)
A flash is a sudden bright light.
A flash of lightning lit up the sky.

56

Extra information
Other words with the same ending

Numbers
Numbers separate different meanings of the same headword.

Guidewords
The first and last words on a page are shown at the top of the page.

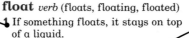

float *verb* (floats, floating, floated)
1 If something floats, it stays on top of a liquid.
2 If something floats through the air, it drifts along gently.
The red balloon floated above the rooftops.
♦ The opposite of float is sink.
Some other words that end with the letters 'oat' are: boat coat goat throat

flat *adjective* (flatter, flattest)
Something that is flat does not slope or have any bumps or wrinkles. The top of a table is flat.
Find something flat to put your paper on.

flat *noun* (flats)
A flat is a home. It is a set of rooms inside a house or big building.
♦ Some other words that end with the letters 'at' are: bat cat hat mat pat rat sat that

flavour *noun* (flavours)
The flavour of food or drink is what it tastes like.
My favourite flavour of ice cream is strawberry.

flock *noun* (flocks)
A flock is a group of birds or sheep.
♦ The word flock comes from an old word that meant 'a crowd of people'.

floor *noun* (floors)
A floor is the part of a room or building that people walk on.
We all sat on the floor watching television.
♦ The part of a room opposite the floor is the ceiling.

flour *noun*
Flour is a powder made from wheat that you use to make bread and cakes.
♦ The word flour sounds just like flower.

flow *verb* (flows, flowing, flowed)
To flow means to move along like water.
The stream flows very fast here.

flower *noun* (flowers)
A flower is the part of a plant that makes seeds. Many flowers are brightly coloured.
♦ The word flower sounds just like flour.
There are many different types of flower. Here are some of them:
bluebell, buttercup, carnation, crocus, daffodil, daisy, dandelion, foxglove, pansy, rose, sunflower, tulip

flew SEE **fly**
A helicopter flew over our heads.

flipper *noun* (flippers)
The flippers on animals such as seals, turtles, or penguins are the flat arms that they use for swimming.

57

a
b
c
d
e
f
g
h
i
j
k
l
m
n
o
p
q
r
s
t
u
v
w
x
y
z

Extra information
Opposites

Alphabet
To help with alphabetical order

Extra information
Word origins

Example sentences
Example sentences show you how to use the word in a sentence.

Other endings
Words often change their endings if they are used in the plural or in a different tense. These different spellings are often shown in black after the word class.

Cross-references
Difficult word classes or parts of speech are included as cross-references.

7

Aa

a

This book is a dictionary.

about

It's a book about words.

I'll be back in about an hour.

above

Above means higher up.

The top of the giant beanstalk was above the clouds.

◆ The opposite of above is below.

accident *noun* (accidents)

An accident is something nasty that was not meant to happen.

He broke his arm in a car accident.

ache *verb* (aches, aching, ached)

If part of your body aches, it keeps on hurting.

The long bicycle ride made my legs ache.

act *verb* (acts, acting, acted)

If you act, you pretend to be someone else in a play, show, or film.

◆ A person who acts in a play, show, or film is called an actor. A female actor is sometimes called an actress.

add *verb* (adds, adding, added)

1 When you add something, you put it with something else.

Mix the eggs and sugar. Then add flour.

2 When you add numbers, you work out how many you get when you put them together.

Three add two equals five.

address

noun (addresses)

Someone's address is the number of their house, and the name of the street and town where they live.

The President,
The White House,
Washington,
U.S.A.

adult *noun* (adults)

An adult is a person or animal that has grown up.

adventure *noun* (adventures)

An adventure is something exciting that happens to you.

Michael, John, and Wendy have many adventures with Peter Pan in Never-Never Land.

aeroplane *noun* (aeroplanes)

An aeroplane is a flying machine with wings, and usually one or more engines.

afraid *adjective*

Someone who is afraid thinks something bad might happen to them.

Are you afraid of the wolf?

◆ Other words that mean the same as afraid are frightened and scared.

after

After means at a later time.

We can go to the park after lunch.

afternoon *noun* (afternoons)

The afternoon is the time from the middle of the day until about six o'clock.

again

Again means one more time.

Can we play that game again?

against

If you are against somebody, you are on the opposite side to them.

We played a game of football, children against grown-ups.

age *noun*

The age of someone or something is how old they are.

agree *verb* (agrees, agreeing, agreed)

If you agree with someone, you think the same as they do.

Tweedledum and Tweedledee agreed to have a battle.

air *noun*

Air is what everyone breathes. It is made of gases that we cannot see.

airport *noun* (airports)

An airport is a place where aeroplanes land and take off.

alive *adjective*

A person, animal, or plant that is alive is living at the moment.

◆ The opposite of alive is dead.

Some other words that end with the letters 'ive' are: dive drive five hive

a
b
c
d
e
f
g
h
i
j
k
l
m
n
o
p
q
r
s
t
u
v
w
x
y
z

9

a
b
c
d
e
f
g
h
i
j
k
l
m
n
o
p
q
r
s
t
u
v
w
x
y
z

all

All means the whole of a group or thing.

All the ducks started quacking.

We ate all the cake.

◆ Some other words that end with the letters 'all' are: ball call fall tall wall

allow *verb* (allows, allowing, allowed)

If someone allows you to do something, they let you do it.

Dogs are not allowed to come in the shop.

almost

Almost means very nearly.

We almost missed the bus.

alone *adjective*

If someone is alone, there is nobody with them.

Our cat has been alone in the house all day.

alphabet *noun* (alphabets)

An alphabet is all the letters that are used in writing, arranged in a special order.

◆ The word alphabet comes from the words alpha and beta, which are the names of the first two letters of the Greek alphabet.

also

Also means as well.

I have a pet rabbit and also two hamsters.

always

If something always happens, it happens every time.

I always have juice and cereal for breakfast.

am

I am hungry.

ambulance *noun* (ambulances)

An ambulance is a special van for taking people to hospital when they are ill or badly hurt.

amphibian *noun* (amphibians)

Amphibians are animals that start their lives in water and later change so they are able to live on land. Frogs and toads are amphibians.

an

There is an ant.

anchor *noun* (anchors)

An anchor is a heavy, metal hook on a long chain. It is dropped to the bottom of the sea to stop a ship from moving.

ancient *adjective*

Things that are ancient are very old.

and

I like spiders and beetles.

angry *adjective* (angrier, angriest)

If you are angry, you are not pleased at all with what someone has done or said.

Dad was angry when I broke the window.

animal *noun* (animals)

An animal is something that lives, can move about, and is not a plant. Elephants, parrots, bees, goldfish, and people are all animals.

ankle *noun* (ankles)

Your ankle is the part where your leg joins your foot.

announce *verb* (announces, announcing, announced)

If people announce something, they tell everyone about it.

The king announced the wedding of Princess Jasmine and Aladdin.

annoy *verb* (annoys, annoying, annoyed)

If someone annoys you, they make you angry.

Josh annoyed his brother by singing the same song over and over again.

another

Another means one more.

Please can I have another biscuit?

answer *verb* (answers, answering, answered)

When you answer, you speak when someone calls you or asks you a question.

'Is anybody there?', said Hollie, but nobody answered.

ant *noun* (ants)

An ant is a tiny insect. Ants live in large groups called colonies.

anteater *noun* (anteaters)

An anteater is an animal with a long tongue that eats ants.

anxious *adjective*

If you are anxious, you feel worried about something.

Little Bo Peep was anxious about her sheep.

any

1 Any means some.

Have you got any ice cream?

2 Any also means whichever one you want.

You can choose any book you like.

anyone

Anyone or anybody means any person.

Does anyone want ice cream?

ape *noun* (apes)

An ape is an animal like a large monkey without a tail. Chimpanzees and gorillas are apes.

◆ Some other words that end with the letters 'ape' are: grape shape tape

appear *verb* (appears, appearing, appeared)

If something appears, you can suddenly see it.

Cinderella's fairy godmother appeared beside her.

◆ The opposite of appear is disappear.

11

a
b
c
d
e
f
g
h
i
j
k
l
m
n
o
p
q
r
s
t
u
v
w
x
y
z

apple *noun* (apples)

An apple is a round, crisp fruit. Apples have green, red, or yellow skins.

apron *noun* (aprons)

A piece of clothing that you wear over your other clothes to keep them clean when you are cooking or painting.

are

Parrots are birds.

area *noun* (areas)

An area is part of a town or place.
We live in a nice area next to the park.

argue *verb* (argues, arguing, argued)

When you argue with somebody, you talk about things you do not agree on.
My brother and I are always arguing.

◆ Another word that means the same as argue is quarrel.

arm *noun* (arms)

Your arm is the part of your body between your shoulder and your hand.

armchair *noun* (armchairs)

An armchair is a comfortable chair with parts at the side to rest your arms on.

◆ Little words can hide in big words. Can you *see* the words arm, chair, hair, and air hiding in the word armchair?

armour *noun*

Armour is a metal suit that soldiers wore a long time ago to protect them in battle.

army *noun* (armies)

An army is a large group of soldiers who are trained to fight on land in a war.

arrange *verb* (arranges, arranging, arranged)

If you arrange things, you put them in order.
Sam arranged the videos neatly.

arrow *noun* (arrows)

An arrow is a pointed stick that you shoot with a bow.

art *noun*

Art is something special that someone has made, like a drawing, painting, or carving.

◆ People who make art are called artists.

as

The lamb was as white as snow.

ask *verb* (asks, asking, asked)

1 When you ask a question, you are trying to find something out.
'What is your name?' Tommy asked.

2 If you ask for something, you say you want it to be given to you.
'Can I have a lolly?' Rachel asked.

asleep *adjective*

When you are asleep, you are resting completely, with your eyes closed, and you don't know what is going on around you.

Sleeping Beauty was asleep for a hundred years.

a
b
c
d
e
f
g
h
i
j
k
l
m
n
o
p
q
r
s
t
u
v
w
x
y
z

assembly *noun* (assemblies)

Assembly is the time when a large group of people meet together.

I was late for school assembly.

astronaut *noun* (astronauts)

An astronaut is a person who travels in space.

◆ The word astronaut comes from two Greek words that mean 'star' and 'sailor'. So an astronaut is really a 'star sailor'.

How do you get a baby astronaut to sleep? Rocket.

at

We had lunch at Grandma's house.

ate SEE **eat**

Goldilocks ate Baby Bear's porridge.

◆ The word ate sounds just like eight.

attack *verb* (attacks, attacking, attacked)

If you attack someone, you try to hurt them.

attention *noun*

When you pay attention to somebody, you listen carefully and think about what they are saying.

James, stop talking and pay attention.

◆ Little words can hide in big words. Can you see the words at, ten, tent, and on hiding in the word attention?

audience *noun* (audiences)

An audience is a group of people who have come to a place to watch or listen to something.

At the end of the play the audience clapped loudly.

aunt *noun* (aunts)

Your aunt is the sister of your mother or father, or the wife of your uncle.

author *noun* (authors)

An author is a person who writes a book or story.

autumn *noun* (autumns)

Autumn is the part of the year when it gets colder, and leaves fall from the trees.

◆ Autumn is between summer and winter.

awake *adjective*

When you are awake, you are not asleep.

Are you awake yet?

away

Away means going to a different place.

At the stroke of midnight, Cinderella ran away from the ball.

Bb

baby *noun* (babies)

A baby is a very young child.

back *noun* (backs)

1 The back of something is the part opposite the front.

Josh sat at the back of the boat.

2 Your back is the part of your body between your neck and your bottom.

◆ Some other words that end with the letters 'ack' are: black crack pack quack sack

bad *adjective* (worse, worst)

1 Things that are bad are not good.

Sugar is bad for your teeth.

2 Bad food is not fit to eat.

◆ Some other words that end with the letters 'ad' are: dad glad had sad

bag *noun* (bags)

A bag is used to hold or carry things.

bake *verb* (bakes, baking, baked)

When you bake something, you cook it in an oven.

My dad is baking a cake for my birthday.

◆ A person who *bakes* and *sells* bread and cakes is called a baker.

balance *verb* (balances, balancing, balanced)

When you balance something, you keep it steady.

Can you balance a ball on your head?

ball *noun* (balls)

A ball is a round object that is used in games.

◆ Some other words that end with the letters 'all' are: all call fall tall wall

14

balloon *noun* (balloons)

A balloon is a rubber bag that you can blow into and make bigger.

banana *noun* (bananas)

A banana is a long, curved fruit with a thick, yellow skin.

band *noun* (bands)

1 A band is a group of people who play musical instruments together.

My brother plays in a steel drum band.

2 A band can also be a strip of material round something.

Tie your hair back with this band.

◆ Some other words that end with the letters 'and' are: hand land sand stand

bank *noun* (banks)

1 A bank is the ground along the side of a river or canal.

Mole and Ratty lived on the river bank.

2 A bank is also a place that looks after money for people.

◆ Why are rivers good places for collecting money?
Because they have banks on either side.

bar *noun* (bars)

A bar is a long, thin piece of wood or metal.

The monkey put its hand through the bars of its cage.

◆ Some other words that end with the letters 'ar' are: car far jar star

bare *adjective* (barer, barest)

1 If part of someone's body is bare, it is not covered with anything.

Mina is dancing in her bare feet.

2 A room or cupboard that is bare has nothing in it.

◆ The word bare sounds just like bear.

bargain *noun* (bargains)

A bargain is something that is worth more than you pay for it.

Two books for the price of one is a real bargain.

bark *noun*

Bark is the hard covering round the trunk and branches of a tree.

bark *verb* (barks, barking, barked)

When dogs bark, they make a sudden, loud sound.

◆ Some other words that end with the letters 'ark' are: dark mark park

barn *noun* (barns)

A barn is a large building on a farm, where a farmer stores things like hay. Animals are sometimes kept in barns at night.

baseball *noun*

Baseball is a game played with a bat and ball. There are nine players on each side.

basket *noun* (baskets)

A basket is for holding or carrying things. Baskets are made of strips of material like straw or thin wood.

'What have you got in your basket?' asked the wolf.

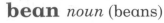

a
b
c
d
e
f
g
h
i
j
k
l
m
n
o
p
q
r
s
t
u
v
w
x
y
z

bat *noun* (bats)

1 A bat is a piece of wood for hitting the ball in a game.

2 A bat is also an animal that looks like a mouse with wings.

◆ Some other words that end with the letters 'at' are: cat flat hat mat pat rat sat that

bath *noun* (baths)

A bath can be filled with water so that you can sit in it and wash yourself.

bathroom *noun* (bathrooms)

A bathroom is a room with a bath or shower.

battery *noun* (batteries)

A battery has electricity inside it. You put batteries in things like watches and radios to make them work.

battle *noun* (battles)

A battle is a fight between armies.

be

Can I be in goal?

beach *noun* (beaches)

A beach is land by the edge of the sea. It is usually covered with sand or small stones.

beak *noun* (beaks)

A beak is the hard part of a bird's mouth.

The bird had some twigs in its beak.

◆ A duck's beak is called a bill.

bean *noun* (beans)

A bean is a large seed of a plant that you can eat as a vegetable.

Jack swapped the cow for some magic beans.

bear *noun* (bears)

A bear is a big, heavy animal with thick fur and sharp claws.

◆ A baby bear is called a cub.

The word bear sounds just like bare.

How do you start a bear race? Ready, Teddy, Go!

beard *noun* (beards)

A beard is the hair that grows on a man's chin and cheeks.

The wizard had a long white beard.

beat *verb* (beats, beating, beat, beaten)

1 If you beat someone in a race or game, you do better than them and win it.

The hare ran very fast, but the tortoise beat him.

2 To beat can also mean to keep hitting with a stick.

Don't let him beat the donkey.

◆ Some other words that end with the letters 'eat' are: eat heat meat neat seat wheat

beautiful *adjective*

You say something is beautiful if you enjoy looking at it or listening to it.

What a beautiful painting!

because

I was late because I missed the bus.

bed *noun* (beds)

A bed is a piece of furniture you sleep on.

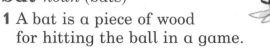

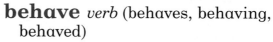

bedroom *noun* (bedrooms)

A bedroom is a room you sleep in.

bedtime *noun*

Bedtime is the time when you usually go to bed.

bee *noun* (bees)

A bee is an insect with wings. Bees make honey.

◆ Bees live in a beehive.

been

Pussy cat, pussy cat, where have you been?

beetle *noun* (beetles)

A beetle is an insect with hard wing-covers.

◆ The word *beetle* comes from an old word that means 'a thing that bites'.

before

Before means at an earlier time.

I brush my teeth before I go to bed.

began SEE **begin**

Tom began to read when he was four.

begin *verb* (begins, beginning, began, begun)

When you begin, you start something.

Begin running when I blow the whistle.

◆ Another word that means the same as begin is start.

The opposite of begin is finish or end or stop.

begun SEE **begin**

I have just begun a new drawing.

behave *verb* (behaves, behaving, behaved)

If someone tells you to behave, they want you to be good.

behind

Behind means at the back of something.

David hid behind a chair.

believe *verb* (believes, believing, believed)

If you believe something, you feel that it is true.

Do you believe in ghosts?

bell *noun* (bells)

A bell is a piece of metal that makes a ringing sound when you hit or shake it.

◆ Some other words that end with the letters 'ell' are: fell sell shell spell tell well yell

belong *verb* (belongs, belonging, belonged)

1 If something belongs to you, it is yours.

That pen belongs to me.

2 If something belongs somewhere, that is its proper place.

Where do these plates belong?

below

Below means lower down.

I sleep on the top bunk and my brother sleeps below.

◆ The opposite of below is above.

belt *noun* (belts)

A belt is a band you wear round your waist.

bench *noun* (benches)

A bench is a long seat for more than one person.

bend *verb* (bends, bending, bent)

If you bend something, you change its shape so it is not straight.

Bend your knees, then straighten them.

bent SEE **bend**

I bent the piece of wire into a circle.

best *adjective*

Something or somebody that is best is better than any of the others.

James is the best player in the team.

◆ The opposite of best is worst.

better

1 If someone can do something better than you, they do it with more skill than you do.

Mum can draw better than Dad can.

2 If one thing is better than another, it is more useful, or nearer to what you want.

Your red coat would be better today — it's warmer.

3 If you are feeling better, you are well again.

I had a bad cough last week, but I'm better now.

◆ The opposite of better is worse.

between

Between means in the middle.

The bear was standing between two trees.

bicycle *noun* (bicycles)

A bicycle is a machine that you can ride. Bicycles have two wheels and pedals which you turn with your feet.

◆ A bicycle is often called a bike for short.

a **b** c d e f g h i j k l m n o p q r s t u v w x y z

big *adjective* (bigger, biggest)
Somebody or something big is large.
An elephant is much bigger than a mouse.
◆ Other words that mean the same as big are enormous, huge, and large.
The opposite of big is small.

bike *noun* (bikes)
A bike is a bicycle.

bin *noun* (bins)
A bin is something to put things in. You can use bins to store things like bread or flour. Some bins are for rubbish.
◆ Some other words that end with the letters 'in' are: chin pin spin thin tin twin win

bird *noun* (birds)
A bird is an animal that has wings, feathers, and a beak. Most birds can fly.
◆ There are many different types of bird. Here are some of them: chicken, dove, duck, eagle, flamingo, owl, parrot, peacock, pelican, penguin, pigeon, puffin, robin, sparrow, swan, woodpecker.

birthday *noun* (birthdays)
Your birthday is the day you were born.
My birthday is 24th November.

biscuit *noun* (biscuits)
A biscuit is a kind of small, thin, dry cake.
◆ What's the difference between a biscuit and an elephant?
You can't dip an elephant in your tea.

bit SEE **bite**
Snow White bit into the apple.

bit *noun* (bits)
A bit is a tiny piece of something.

bite *verb* (bites, biting, bit, bitten)
If you bite something, you use your teeth to cut into it.
◆ Some other words that end with the letters 'ite' are: kite white write

bitten SEE **bite**
The parrot has bitten my finger.

a
b
c
d
e
f
g
h
i
j
k
l
m
n
o
p
q
r
s
t
u
v
w
x
y
z

black *adjective*

Black is the darkest colour.

◆ Some other words that end with the letters 'ack' are: back crack pack quack sack

blade *noun* (blades)

A blade is the flat, sharp part of a knife or sword.

blame *verb* (blames, blaming, blamed)

If you blame someone, you think it is because of them that something bad has happened.

Mum always blames me if the room gets messy.

◆ Some other words that end with the letters 'ame' are: flame frame game name same tame

blanket *noun* (blankets)

A blanket is a thick cover for a bed.

blew SEE **blow**

The big bad wolf blew down the little pig's house.

blind *adjective*

Someone who is blind cannot see at all.

blind *noun* (blinds)

A blind is something you pull down to cover a window.

block *noun* (blocks)

A block is a thick piece of something solid like wood or stone.

block *verb* (blocks, blocking, blocked)

If something is blocked, things cannot get through.

Large trucks blocked the road.

blood *noun*

Blood is the red liquid that moves round inside your body.

blow *verb* (blows, blowing, blew, blown)

1 When you blow, you make air come out of your mouth.

See if you can blow the candles out.

2 When the wind blows, it moves the air.

The wind is blowing the leaves off the trees.

blown SEE **blow**

I've already blown the balloons up.

blue *adjective*

Blue is the colour of the sky on a sunny day.

The wizard had a large blue hat.

blunt (blunter, bluntest)

Something like a knife or a pencil that is blunt is not sharp.

◆ The opposite of blunt is sharp.

boat *noun* (boats)

A boat floats and carries people or things on water.

◆ Some other words that end with the letters 'oat' are: coat float goat throat

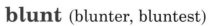

body *noun* (bodies)

The body of a person or animal is the whole of them.

The monster's body was covered in blue spots.

boil *verb* (boils, boiling, boiled)

1 When water boils, it is very hot and you can see bubbles and steam.

2 When you boil something, you cook it in boiling water.

It's time to boil the potatoes.

bone *noun* (bones)

Your bones are the hard white parts inside your body.

◆ All the bones in your body join together to make your skeleton.

bonfire *noun* (bonfires)

A bonfire is a large fire that someone lights outdoors.

book *noun* (books)

A book has pages fixed inside a cover. Books have writing or pictures in them.

Mina was reading a book about castles.

◆ Some other words that end with the letters 'ook' are: cook hook look took

boot *noun* (boots)

1 A boot is a kind of shoe that comes up above your ankle.

We put our boots on and went out to build a snowman.

2 A boot is also the place in a car where you put luggage.

Put your skateboard in the boot.

bored *adjective*

If you are bored, you feel tired or irritated because you have nothing to do.

boring *adjective*

If something is boring, it is not interesting.

born

When a baby is born, it comes out of its mother's body.

My baby brother was born last week.

borrow *verb* (borrows, borrowing, borrowed)

When you borrow something from somebody, you take it for a short time and promise to give it back later.

Can I borrow your pencil?

◆ The opposite of borrow is lend.

both

Both means the two of them, not just one.

Use both hands to carry that heavy dish.

bottle *noun* (bottles)

A bottle is made to hold liquids. Bottles are made of glass or plastic.

bottom *noun* (bottoms)

1 The bottom is the lowest part of anything.

Jill rolled down to the bottom of the hill.

2 Your bottom is the part of your body that you sit on.

◆ The opposite of the first meaning of bottom is top.

bought SEE **buy**

My Dad bought me a new bike.

bounce *verb* (bounces, bouncing, bounced)

When something bounces, it comes back again after hitting something else.

Tigger bounced into the room.

a
b
c
d
e
f
g
h
i
j
k
l
m
n
o
p
q
r
s
t
u
v
w
x
y
z

bow *noun* (bows)

1 A bow is a knot you use to tie a ribbon.
Katie tied a big red bow around the box.

2 A bow is also a bent piece of wood used for shooting arrows.

◆ This word rhymes with go.

bow *verb* (bows, bowing, bowed)

If you bow, you bend over at the waist.
The red knight bowed to the king.

◆ This word rhymes with cow.

bowl *noun* (bowls)

A bowl is a kind of deep plate that is made to hold things like soup, fruit, or breakfast cereals.
Goldilocks found three bowls of porridge.

22

box *noun* (boxes)

A box has straight sides and is made to hold things. Most boxes are made from cardboard, wood, or plastic.

boy *noun* (boys)

A boy is a male child or young adult.

Pinocchio was a wooden puppet who wanted to be a real boy.

brain *noun* (brains)

Your brain is inside your head. You use your brain for thinking, remembering, and having feelings.

◆ Some other words that end with the letters 'ain' are: chain drain grain main pain rain train

branch *noun* (branches)

A branch grows out from the trunk of a tree.

Look, there's a robin sitting on a branch.

brave *adjective* (braver, bravest)

If you are brave, you show that you are not afraid.

The young princess was brave to fight the dragon alone.

bread *noun*

Bread is a food made by baking flour mixed with water.

break *verb* (breaks, breaking, broke, broken)

If something breaks, it goes into pieces or stops working.

Be careful, Dad, or you'll break a window with that ball.

breakfast *noun* (breakfasts)

Breakfast is the first meal after you wake up in the morning.

The three bears sat down to breakfast.

◆ The word breakfast comes from the words break which means 'to end' and fast which means 'a time when you don't eat anything'. So when you wake up in the morning you break your fast by eating breakfast.

breathe *verb* (breathes, breathing, breathed)

When you breathe, you take air in through your nose or mouth and then let it out again.

The dragon was breathing fire and smoke.

brick *noun* (bricks)

A brick is a small block of baked clay. Bricks are used for building.

◆ Some other words that end with the letters 'ick' are: chick click flick kick lick pick quick sick stick thick trick

a
b
c
d
e
f
g
h
i
j
k
l
m
n
o
p
q
r
s
t
u
v
w
x
y
z

23

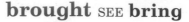

a
b
c
d
e
f
g
h
i
j
k
l
m
n
o
p
q
r
s
t
u
v
w
x
y

bridge *noun* (bridges)

A bridge goes over a river, railway, or road, so that people or traffic can get across.

A horrible troll lived under the bridge.

bright *adjective* (brighter, brightest)

1 Bright colours are strong and easy to see.

2 Bright lights shine strongly.

3 A person who is bright learns quickly.

◆ Some other words that end with the letters 'ight' are: fight fright light night right tight

bring *verb* (brings, bringing, brought)

If you bring something, you carry it here.

Don't forget to bring some food for our picnic.

◆ Some other words that end with the letters 'ing' are: King ring sing sting string swing thing wing

broke SEE **break**

I dropped my glass and broke it.

broken SEE **break**

Jamie has broken my watch.

broom *noun* (brooms)

A broom is a brush with a long handle. It is used for sweeping a floor or path.

brother *noun* (brothers)

Your brother is a boy who has the same parents as you do.

brought SEE **bring**

I have brought you some flowers.

brown *adjective*

Brown is the colour of chocolate, wood, and soil.

◆ Some other words that end with the letters 'own' are: clown crown down frown town

brush *noun* (brushes)

A brush has lots of short stiff hairs, fixed into a handle made of wood or plastic.

◆ You use a hairbrush to make your hair tidy. You use a toothbrush to clean your teeth. You use a paintbrush to paint with.

bubble *noun* (bubbles)

A bubble is a small ball of soap or liquid with air inside.

Jenny was blowing bubbles.

bucket *noun* (buckets)

A bucket has a handle and is used to carry liquids or sand.

build *verb* (builds, building, built)

If you build something, you make it by putting different parts together.

The men are building a brick house.

building *noun* (buildings)

A building has walls and a roof. Houses, factories, and schools are buildings.

built SEE **build**

A bird built a nest in the old tree.

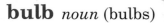

bulb *noun* (bulbs)

1 A bulb is the glass part of a lamp that gives light.

2 A bulb can also be the root of a flower. Daffodils and tulips grow from bulbs.

bull *noun* (bulls)

A bull is a large male animal of the cow family.

◆ What do you call a sleeping bull? A *bulldozer.*

bulldozer *noun* (bulldozers)

A bulldozer is a machine with a wide piece of metal at the front. It is used to push heavy rocks and soil out of the way.

bump *noun* (bumps)

A bump is a round lump on something.

There was a bump in the road where it went over the bridge.

burn *verb* (burns, burning, burnt, burned)

1 If something is burning, it is on fire.

The bonfire was burning brightly.

2 If someone burns something, they damage it with fire or heat.

Try not to burn the toast this time.

burst *verb* (bursts, bursting, burst)

When something bursts, it breaks open suddenly.

The bag burst and all the oranges fell onto the floor.

bus *noun* (buses)

Buses are big vehicles that can carry lots of people to and from places.

bush *noun* (bushes)

A bush is like a small tree, with lots of branches.

busy *adjective* (busier, busiest)

1 Someone who is busy has a lot to do.

I can't help you just yet — I'm busy.

2 When a place is busy, there's a lot going on.

The supermarket was busy today.

but

The front door was open, but there was nobody in the house.

butter *noun*

Butter is a yellow food that is made from cream. You can spread it on bread or cook with it.

butterfly *noun* (butterflies)

A butterfly is an insect with four large wings.

button *noun* (buttons)

Buttons are small, round objects sewn on to clothes. They fit into holes or loops to keep clothes done up.

buy *verb* (buys, buying, bought)

When you buy something, you pay money to have it.

I'd like to buy a dinosaur poster.

◆ The opposite of buy is *sell*.

buzz *verb* (buzzes, buzzing, buzzed)

If something buzzes, it makes a humming sound like a bee makes.

by

Let's sit by the fire.

a
b
c
d
e
f
g
h
i
j
k
l
m
n
o
p
q
r
s
t
u
v
w
x
y
z

Cc

cage *noun* (cages)

A cage is a box or room with bars. Pets like mice and gerbils live in cages.

cake *noun* (cakes)

A cake is food made with flour, butter, eggs, and sugar. You bake a cake in the oven.

calculator *noun* (calculators)

A calculator is a machine that you use to solve maths problems.

◆ How do you count cows?
With a cowculator.

calendar *noun* (calendars)

A calendar is a list showing all the days, weeks, and months in a year.

Look, I've marked everyone's birthday on the calendar.

calf *noun* (calves)

1 A calf is a young cow or bull.

2 Your calf is at the back of your leg, between your knee and your ankle.

call *verb* (calls, calling, called)

1 If you call someone, you speak loudly so that they will come to you.

Didn't you hear me call you?

2 If a person or thing is called something, that is their name.

We have a dog called Razzle.

◆ Some other words that end with the letters 'all' are: all ball fall tall wall

came SEE **come**

All my friends came for a sleepover.

camel *noun* (camels)

A camel is a big animal with one or two humps on its back. Camels can carry people and things across deserts.

camera *noun* (cameras)

You use a camera to take photos.

camp *noun* (camps)

A camp is a group of tents or huts where people live for a short time.

can *verb*

If you can do something, you are able to do it.

Run, run, as fast as you can!

can *noun* (cans)

A can is made of metal. You can buy food or drinks in cans.

◆ Some other words that end with the letters 'an' are: man pan ran van

canal *noun* (canals)

A canal is a type of river that has been specially made for boats to travel along.

candle *noun* (candles)

A candle is a stick of wax with string through the middle. You can set the string on fire and it gives light.

◆ The word candle comes from a Latin word that means 'to shine'.

canoe *noun* (canoes)

A canoe is a long, narrow boat. You move it through the water with short oars called paddles.

◆ If you mix up all the letters in the word canoe, you can make the word ocean.

can't *verb*

If you can't do something, you are not able to do it.

You can't catch me, I'm the Gingerbread Man!

car *noun* (cars)

You can ride in a car. It has wheels and an engine to make it go.

My dad goes to work in the car.

◆ These are different parts of a car: bonnet, boot, door, engine, headlight, roof, tyre, wheel, windscreen.

Some other words that end with the letters 'ar' are: bar far jar star

card *noun* (cards)

1 Card is thick, stiff paper.

2 A greetings card has a picture and words on it. You send cards to people at special times, like birthdays.

When I was ill, I got lots of cards.

3 Playing cards have numbers or pictures on them. You play games with them.

a
b
c
d
e
f
g
h
i
j
k
l
m
n
o
p
q
r
s
t
u
v
w
x
y
z

a
b
c
d
e
f
g
h
i
j
k
l
m
n
o
p
q
r
s
t
u
v
w
x
y
z

cardboard *noun*

Cardboard is very thick, strong paper.

Robbie carried the kittens in a cardboard box.

care *verb* (cares, caring, cared)

1 If you care for something, you look after it.

My grandpa taught me how to care for pet fish.

2 If you care about something, you think it matters.

She cares a lot about her pencils.

careful *adjective*

If you are careful, you think about what you are doing and try to do it safely and well.

Be careful when you cross the road.

careless *adjective*

If you are careless, you do not think enough about what you are doing.

carpet *noun* (carpets)

A carpet is a thick cover for the floor.

carrot *noun* (carrots)

A carrot is a long, orange vegetable. Carrots grow under the ground.

carry *verb* (carries, carrying, carried)

If you carry something, you take it from one place to another.

The lion carried the cub in its mouth.

carton *noun* (cartons)

A carton is made of thin cardboard or plastic. You can buy food or drinks in cartons.

We need to buy a carton of milk.

cartoon *noun* (cartoons)

1 A cartoon is a film that uses drawings instead of actors.

There's a Tom and Jerry cartoon on soon.

2 A cartoon is also a funny drawing.

case *noun* (cases)

You can keep or carry things in a case. There are cases to hold things like pencils or clothes.

I've packed my case already.

castle *noun* (castles)

A castle is a large, strong building with very thick stone walls and tall towers. Castles were built long ago to keep the people inside safe from their enemies.

cat *noun* (cats)

A cat is a furry animal. Small cats are often kept as pets. Large cats like lions and tigers live in the wild.

◆ A baby cat is called a kitten. A baby lion or tiger is called a cub.

Some other words that end with the letters 'at' are: bat flat hat mat pat rat sat that

catch *verb* (catches, catching, caught)

1 When you catch something that is moving, you get hold of it.

You can't catch me, I'm the Gingerbread Man!

2 If you catch a bus, you are on time to get on it.

3 If you catch an illness, you become ill with it.

I hope you don't catch my cold.

caterpillar *noun* (caterpillars)

A caterpillar is a long, creeping creature that will turn into a butterfly or moth.

◆ Little words can hide in big words. Can you see the words cat, at, ate, pill, and ill hiding in the word caterpillar?

caught SEE **catch**

Katie caught the kitten with both hands.

cave *noun* (caves)

A cave is a big hole under the ground or inside a mountain.

Deep in the cave, Ali Baba found a pile of treasure.

CD *noun* (CDs)

CD is short for compact disc. CDs hold music or information. You play them on a CD player or computer.

ceiling *noun* (ceilings)

A ceiling is the part of a room above your head.

centipede *noun* (centipedes)

A centipede is a creature that looks like a hairy worm with lots of tiny legs.

◆ The word centipede comes from two Latin words that mean 'a hundred feet'.

cereal *noun* (cereals)

1 A cereal is a kind of grass grown by farmers for its seeds.

Rice, wheat, and oats are cereals.

2 A cereal is also a kind of breakfast food that you eat with milk.

chain *noun* (chains)

A chain is a number of rings joined together in a line.

◆ Some other words that end with the letters 'ain' are: brain drain grain main pain rain train

chair *noun* (chairs)

A chair is a seat with a back and sometimes arms, for one person.

◆ Some other words that end with the letters 'air' are: air fair hair stair

a
b
c
d
e
f
g
h
i
j
k
l
m
n
o
p
q
r
s
t
u
v
w
x
y
z

29

a
b
c
d
e
f
g
h
i
j
k
l
m
n
o
p
q
r
s
t
u
v
w
x
y
z

chalk *noun* (chalks)

1 Chalk is a soft white rock.
The cliffs here are made of chalk.

2 Chalks are pieces of soft white rock that you write or draw with on a blackboard.

change *verb* (changes, changing, changed)

When things change, they become different.
As tadpoles grow, they change into frogs.

change *noun*

Change is the money you get back when you have paid more than something costs.
I haven't got the right money. Can you give me change?

channel *noun* (channels)

1 A channel is a narrow ditch for water.

2 You have different channels on your television set. Each one has its own programmes.

chapter *noun* (chapters)

A chapter is a part of a book.
Chapter 5 is all about the planets.

charge *noun*

Someone who is in charge of something makes sure that it is looked after.
Mrs Dodds is in charge of the library at school.

charge *verb* (charges, charging, charged)

If someone charges you for something, they ask you to pay money for it.
Does the zoo charge for children to go in?

chase *verb* (chases, chasing, chased)

When you chase somebody, you run after them and try to catch them.
Our cat is always chasing birds.

cheap *adjective* (cheaper, cheapest)

Something cheap does not cost very much money.
I like the red shoes, but the blue ones are cheaper.

◆ The opposite of cheap is expensive.

checkout *noun* (checkouts)

A checkout is a place in a supermarket where you pay for things.

cheek *noun* (cheeks)

Your cheeks are the soft parts on each side of your face.
A hamster has places inside its cheeks where it can hold food.

cheer *verb* (cheers, cheering, cheered)

When people cheer, they shout to show they like something.
At the end of the pantomime, everyone cheered and clapped.

cheese *noun*

Cheese is a food. There are lots of different kinds of cheese, but they are all made from milk.
A little mouse was nibbling a piece of cheese.

cheetah *noun* (cheetahs)

A cheetah is a big wild cat with spots on its coat. Cheetahs are the world's fastest animals on land.

cherry *noun* (cherries)

A cherry is a small red or black fruit with a stone in the middle.

chest *noun* (chests)

1 Your chest is the front part of your body, between your neck and your stomach.

2 A chest is a big, strong box with a lid.

chew *verb* (chews, chewing, chewed)

When you chew food, you use your teeth to break it up into smaller pieces.

chick *noun* (chicks)

A chick is a baby bird.

◆ Some other words that end with the letters 'ick' are: brick click flick kick lick pick quick sick stick thick trick

chicken *noun* (chickens)

A chicken is a bird that farmers keep. Chickens lay eggs that we eat.

◆ A female chicken is called a hen. A male chicken is called a cockerel. A baby chicken is called a chick.

child *noun* (children)

A child is a young boy or girl.

chimney *noun* (chimneys)

A chimney is a long pipe that takes smoke from a fire up through the roof of a building.

chin *noun* (chins)

Your chin is the part of your face that is below your mouth.

◆ Some other words that end with the letters 'in' are: bin pin spin thin tin twin win

chip *noun* (chips)

A chip is a long, thin piece of potato fried in oil.

chocolate *noun* (chocolates)

Chocolate is a sweet brown food or drink made from cocoa.

choose *verb* (chooses, choosing, chose, chosen)

If you choose something, you make up your mind which one you want.

I couldn't decide which cake to choose.

chop *verb* (chops, chopping, chopped)

If you chop something, you cut it up with an axe or knife.

When Jack reached the ground, he took an axe and chopped down the beanstalk.

chose SEE **choose**

Goldilocks chose the smallest bed.

chosen SEE **choose**

Have you chosen your pizza yet?

church *noun* (churches)

A church is a place where Christian people go to pray.

circle *noun* (circles)

A circle is a round shape like a ring.

circus *noun* (circuses)

A circus is a show in a big tent with clowns, acrobats, and sometimes animals that have been trained to do tricks.

◆ The word circus comes from a Latin word that means 'a ring', because a circus is usually held in a ring-shaped place in a tent.

a
b
c
d
e
f
g
h
i
j
k
l
m
n
o
p
q
r
s
t
u
v
w
x
y
z

a
b
c
d
e
f
g
h
i
j
k
l
m
n
o
p
q
r
s
t
u
v
w
x
y
z

city *noun* (cities)

A city is a very big town.

London and New York are cities.

clap *verb* (claps, clapping, clapped)

If you clap, you hit your hands together to make a noise.

Everyone started to clap at the end of the magic show.

class *noun* (classes)

A class is a group of pupils who learn together.

claw *noun* (claws)

A claw is the sharp, curved nail on the foot of an animal or bird.

clean *adjective* (cleaner, cleanest)

Something that is clean has no dirty marks on it.

This floor is not very clean.

◆ The opposite of clean is dirty.

clean *verb* (cleans, cleaning, cleaned)

When you clean something, you get all the dirt off it.

Snow White cleaned the cottage from top to bottom.

clear *adjective* (clearer, clearest)

1 If something is clear, it is easy to see, hear, or understand.

I found my way easily because the map was so clear.

2 If something is clear, it is free of things you do not want.

If the road is clear, you can cross.

3 If something like glass or plastic is clear, you can see through it.

The water is so clear, you can see the bottom of the pond.

clear *verb* (clears, clearing, cleared)

When you clear a place, you take things away.

I'll help you clear the table.

clever *adjective* (cleverer, cleverest)

Someone who is clever can learn and understand things easily.

Micky is a very clever monkey.

click *noun* (clicks)

A click is a short, sharp sound like the sound an electric light switch makes.

◆ Some other words that end with the letters 'ick' are: brick chick flick kick lick pick quick sick stick thick trick

cliff *noun* (cliffs)

A cliff is a hill with one side that goes straight down. Cliffs are often near the sea.

climb *verb* (climbs, climbing, climbed)

When you climb, you go up or down something high.

The children are climbing the coconut trees again.

cloak *noun* (cloaks)

A cloak is a very loose coat without sleeves.

clock *noun* (clocks)

A clock is a machine that shows you what the time is.

close *adjective* (closer, closest)

When something is close, it is near.

The spider was close to Miss Muffet.

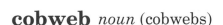

close *verb* (closes, closing, closed)
When you close something, you shut it.
Close your eyes and count to ten.
◆ The opposite of close is open.

cloth *noun* (cloths)
1 Cloth is material for making things like clothes and curtains.
2 A cloth is a piece of cloth for cleaning or covering something.

clothes *noun*
Clothes are the things that people wear.

cloud *noun* (clouds)
1 You can see clouds floating in the sky. They can be white or grey. Clouds are made of tiny drops of water that sometimes fall as rain.
2 Clouds can also be made of dust, smoke, or steam.
Clouds of smoke rose from the bonfire.

clown *noun* (clowns)
A clown wears funny clothes, has a painted face, and does silly things to make people laugh.
◆ Some other words that end with the letters 'own' are: brown crown down frown town

coal *noun*
Coal is black rock that people burn to make heat. Coal comes from under the ground.

coat *noun* (coats)
You put a coat on top of other clothes when you go outside. Coats have long sleeves.
◆ Some other words that end with the letters 'oat' are: boat float goat throat

cobweb *noun* (cobwebs)
A cobweb is a thin, sticky net made by a spider to catch insects.

cocoa *noun*
Cocoa is a brown powder that is used to make chocolate, or a hot drink.

coconut *noun* (coconuts)
A coconut is a large nut with a hard, hairy shell on the outside and a sweet, white part you can eat on the inside.
◆ The word coconut comes from a Spanish word that means 'a grinning face', because this is what the bottom of a coconut shell looks like.

coin *noun* (coins)
A coin is a piece of metal money.

cold *adjective* (colder, coldest)
If you are cold, you feel that you want to put on warm clothes, or stand near something warm.
The weather got very cold and it began to snow.
◆ The opposite of cold is hot.

cold *noun* (colds)
A cold is an illness that makes you sneeze and your nose run.
◆ Some other words that end with the letters 'old' are: bold fold gold hold old sold told

a
b
c
d
e
f
g
h
i
j
k
l
m
n
o
p
q
r
s
t
u
v
w
x
y
z

collar *noun* (collars)

1 A collar is the part that goes round the neck of clothes like shirts and jackets.

2 A collar is also a band that goes round the neck of a dog or cat.

Our dog has a red collar.

colour *noun* (colours)

Red, blue, and yellow are all colours. You can mix these together to get other colours.

You get the colour orange by mixing red and yellow.

come *verb* (comes, coming, came, come)

If you come to a place, you go towards it or arrive there.

Look, the ducks are coming towards us.

comfortable *adjective*

If something is comfortable, it feels good to be in or to wear.

This chair is really comfortable.

comic *noun* (comics)

A comic is a paper with stories told in pictures.

computer *noun* (computers)

A computer is a machine that stores information. Computers can also work things out, or help other machines to work.

control *verb* (controls, controlling, controlled)

If you control something, you are in charge of it and make it do what you want.

Please try to control your dog.

cook *verb* (cooks, cooking, cooked)

If someone cooks food, they get it ready to eat by heating it.

Let's cook pancakes today.

◆ Some other words that end with the letters 'ook' are: book hook look took

cooker *noun* (cookers)

A cooker is a machine for cooking food. It has an oven below for baking, and places on top for boiling or frying.

cool *adjective* (cooler, coolest)

If something is cool, it feels fairly cold.

I'll put the milk in the fridge to keep it cool.

◆ The opposite of cool is warm.

copy *verb* (copies, copying, copied)

If you copy something, you do it exactly the same.

See if you can copy this picture of a horse.

corner *noun* (corners)

A corner is the point where two sides, edges, or streets meet.

Little Jack Horner sat in the corner.

cost *verb* (costs, costing, cost)

If something costs a particular amount, that is how much you have to pay to buy it.

How much does this football cost?

cot *noun* (cots)

A cot is a bed for a baby. Cots have high sides to stop the baby falling out.

cottage *noun* (cottages)

A cottage is a small house in the country.

cotton *noun*

1 Cotton is a light material made from threads of the cotton plant.

My shirt is made of cotton.

2 Cotton is also a thread for sewing.

cough *verb* (coughs, coughing, coughed)

When you cough, you make a sudden loud noise with your throat.

Smoke from the bonfire made us cough.

could *verb*

Nadeen could swim when she was six.

count *verb* (counts, counting, counted)

1 When you count, you say numbers in order.

You count up to fifty, and I'll hide.

2 To count also means to use numbers to find out how many people or things there are.

The farmer is counting his sheep.

country *noun* (countries)

1 A country is a land with its own people and laws.

France, the United States of America, and China are all countries.

2 The country is land with farms and villages away from towns.

cousin *noun* (cousins)

Your cousin is the son or daughter of your aunt or uncle.

cover *verb* (covers, covering, covered)

If you cover something, you put another thing over or round it.

Before we have tea, cover the table with a cloth.

cover *noun* (covers)

A cover is something that goes over or around something else.

The book has a yellow cover.

cow *noun* (cows)

A cow is a large female animal that gives milk.

◆ The male animal is called a bull. A baby cow or bull is called a calf.

crack *noun* (cracks)

1 A crack is a thin line on something where it has broken but not come to pieces.

There is a crack in this cup.

2 A crack is also a sharp noise like the noise a dry twig makes when it breaks.

◆ Some other words that end with the letters 'ack' are: back black pack quack sack

cracker *noun* (crackers)

1 A cracker is a thin biscuit.

2 A cracker is also a paper tube which bangs when two people pull it.

Our Christmas crackers had paper hats and jokes inside.

crane *noun* (cranes)

1 A crane is a tall machine that lifts very heavy things.

2 A crane is also a large bird with very long legs. Cranes live near water.

a
b
c
d
e
f
g
h
i
j
k
l
m
n
o
p
q
r
s
t
u
v
w
x
y
z

a b **c** d e f g h i j k l m n o p q r s t u v w x y z

crash *verb* (crashes, crashing, crashed)

When something crashes, it falls or hits something else with a loud noise.

Huge waves crashed against the side of the ship.

crash *noun* (crashes)

1 A crash is a very loud noise.

The lightning was followed by a crash of thunder.

2 A crash is also a traffic accident.

crawl *verb* (crawls, crawling, crawled)

When you crawl, you move along on your hands and knees.

My little brother can crawl now.

crayon *noun* (crayons)

A crayon is a coloured pencil often made of wax.

cream *noun*

Cream is the thick, fatty part of milk, often used in cakes and puddings.

creature *noun* (creatures)

A creature is any animal.

This forest is full of strange creatures.

creep *verb* (creeps, creeping, crept)

1 If you creep somewhere, you walk very slowly and quietly so no one will hear you.

I saw you creeping down the stairs.

2 An animal that creeps moves along close to the ground.

A caterpillar was creeping up a stem.

crept SEE **creep**

We were late and crept in at the back.

crew *noun* (crews)

A crew is the group of people who work on a ship or aeroplane.

cricket *noun* (crickets)

1 Cricket is a game played with a bat and ball. There are eleven players on each side.

2 A cricket is a jumping insect that makes a shrill sound.

crisp *noun* (crisps)

A crisp is a very thin, dry slice of fried potato.

May I have a packet of crisps please?

crisp *adjective* (crisper, crispest)

1 Things like biscuits that are crisp are dry and break easily.

2 Crisp fruit is firm and fresh.

crocodile *noun* (crocodiles)

A crocodile is a large reptile that lives in rivers in some hot countries.

◆ The word crocodile comes from a Greek word that means 'a lizard'.

What's a crocodile's favourite game? Snap.

crop *noun* (crops)

Crops are the plants that a farmer grows and sells for food.

cross *adjective* (crosser, crossest)

If you are cross, you feel annoyed about something.

cross *noun* (crosses)

A cross is a mark like this + or this ×.

cross *verb* (crosses, crossing, crossed)

If you cross something like a river or road, you go from one side to the other.

'Who dares to cross my bridge?' said the troll.

crowd *noun* (crowds)

A crowd is lots of people in one place.

crown *noun* (crowns)

A crown is a ring of gold and jewels that kings and queens wear on their heads.

The lion and the unicorn were fighting for the crown.

◆ Some other words that end with the letters 'own' are: brown clown down frown town

crust *noun* (crusts)

A crust is the hard part on the outside of bread.

cry *verb* (cries, crying, cried)

When you cry, tears fall from your eyes. People cry when they are sad or hurt.

cry *noun* (cries)

A cry is a shout.

Tom heard a cry and ran to look.

cub *noun* (cubs)

A cub is a young wild animal, especially a young lion, tiger, bear, or fox.

cuddle *verb* (cuddles, cuddling, cuddled)

If you cuddle someone, you hold them closely in your arms.

It's my turn to cuddle the crocodile!

cup *noun* (cups)

People drink things like tea from a cup. A cup has a handle.

cupboard *noun* (cupboards)

A cupboard is a piece of furniture with a door at the front. You keep things in a cupboard.

Old Mother Hubbard went to the cupboard, to fetch her poor dog a bone.

◆ Little words can hide in big words. Can you see the words cup, up, board, and oar hiding in the word cupboard?

curl *noun* (curls)

Curls are pieces of hair that grow or are twisted into rings.

curl *verb* (curls, curling, curled)

If you curl up, you sit or lie with your body bent round itself.

The cat curled up in front of the fire.

◆ Hair with lots of curls in it is curly.

curtain *noun* (curtains)

A curtain is a piece of cloth that you pull across a window to cover it.

curved *adjective*

Something that is curved is not straight.

A parrot has a curved beak.

cut *verb* (cuts, cutting, cut)

If you cut something, you use scissors or a knife.

I'll cut a piece of birthday cake for you.

cut *noun* (cuts)

A cut is an opening in your skin made by something sharp.

a
b
c
d
e
f
g
h
i
j
k
l
m
n
o
p
q
r
s
t
u
v
w
x
y
z

a b **d** e f g h i j k l m n o p q r s t u v w x y z

Dd

dad *noun* (dads)

Dad or daddy is what you call your father.

◆ Some other words that end with the letters 'ad' are: bad glad had sad

damage *verb* (damages, damaging, damaged)

If a person or thing damages something, they spoil it in some way.

The storm damaged lots of trees.

damp *adjective* (damper, dampest)

Something that is damp is a little bit wet.

My towel still feels damp.

dance *verb* (dances, dancing, danced)

When you dance, you move about in time to music.

danger *noun* (dangers)

If there is danger, something bad might happen.

The sign by the pond said 'Danger — thin ice!'

dangerous *adjective*

Something that is dangerous is likely to hurt you.

Crossing a busy road is dangerous.

dark *adjective* (darker, darkest)

1 If it is dark, there is no light or not much light.

We'll need a torch. It's dark outside.

2 Dark hair is brown or black.

◆ The opposite of dark is light.

date *noun* (dates)

1 A date is the day, month, and sometimes the year when something happens.

Today's date is 12th June.

2 A date is also a sticky, brown fruit that grows on a palm tree.

◆ Some other words that end with the letters 'ate' are: gate hate late plate

daughter *noun* (daughters)

A person's daughter is their female child.

The king had three daughters.

day *noun* (days)

1 The day is the time when it is light, from when the sun comes up to when the sun goes down.

I've been working hard all day.

2 A day is the twenty-four hours between one midnight and the next.

◆ The seven days of the week are Sunday, Monday, Tuesday, Wednesday, Thursday, Friday, and Saturday.

Some other words that end with the letters 'ay' are: hay lay may pay play ray say stay way

dead *adjective*

If someone or something is dead, they are no longer living.

Dead leaves had fallen from the trees in the park.

◆ The opposite of dead is alive.

deaf *adjective* (deafer, deafest)

Someone who is deaf cannot hear well. Some deaf people cannot hear at all.

dear *adjective* (dearer, dearest)

Someone who is dear to you is a person you love.

◆ You begin a letter by writing the word Dear before the name of the person you are writing to.

The word dear sounds just like deer.

decide *verb* (decides, deciding, decided)

When you decide, you make up your mind about something.

I can't decide what to wear.

deck *noun* (decks)

A deck is one of the floors on a ship or bus.

decorate *verb* (decorates, decorating, decorated)

1 When you decorate something, you make it look pretty.

We decorated the tree with tinsel and lights.

2 When people decorate a room, they make it look fresh by painting it or putting paper on the walls.

deep *adjective* (deeper, deepest)

Something that is deep goes a long way down from the top.

I'm not allowed in the deep end of the swimming pool.

◆ The opposite of deep is shallow.

a
b
c
d
e
f
g
h
i
j
k
l
m
n
o
p
q
r
s
t
u
v
w
x
y
z

deer *noun* (deer)

A deer is a large animal that can run very fast. Male deer have big horns like branches on their heads, called antlers.

◆ A male deer is called a stag. A female deer is called a doe. A baby deer is called a fawn.

The word deer sounds just like dear.

defend *verb* (defends, defending, defended)

To defend means to keep someone or something safe from attack.

The knights bravely defended the castle.

delicious *adjective*

If something is delicious, it tastes or smells very nice.

deliver *verb* (delivers, delivering, delivered)

If someone delivers something, they bring it to you.

The postman delivered a parcel this morning.

dentist *noun* (dentists)

A dentist's job is to take care of people's teeth.

describe *verb* (describes, describing, described)

If you describe something, you say what it is like.

desert *noun* (deserts)

A desert is a hot, dry land where few plants can grow.

desk *noun* (desks)

A desk is a kind of table where you can read, write, draw, or use a computer.

destroy *verb* (destroys, destroying, destroyed)

If you destroy something, you damage it so much that it can no longer be used.

The bridge was destroyed by the storm.

diamond *noun* (diamonds)

A diamond is a hard, sparkling jewel that is clear like glass.

diary *noun* (diaries)

A diary is a book in which you can write down what happens each day.

dice *noun* (dice)

Dice are small cubes with dots on each face. You throw dice in some games.

It's your turn to throw the dice.

◆ Some other words that end with the letters 'ice' are: ice mice nice price rice

dictionary *noun* (dictionaries)

A dictionary is a book where you can find out what a word means and how to spell it. The words in a dictionary are usually listed in alphabetical order.

did SEE **do**

Did you find your paints?

die *verb* (dies, dying, died)

When a person, animal, or plant dies, they stop living.

Plants die when they don't have enough water.

different *adjective*

If something is different from something else, it is not the same.

All the pencils in the box are different colours.

dinosaur *noun* (dinosaurs)

A dinosaur is a large reptile that lived millions of years ago.

◆ The word dinosaur comes from two Greek words that mean 'terrible lizard'.

There were many different types of dinosaur. Here are some of them: ankylosaurus, brachiosaurus, diplodocus, plesiosaurus, stegosaurus, triceratops, tyrannosaurus rex.

difficult *adjective*

Something that is difficult is not easy to do or understand.

This is a difficult tune to play on the piano.

◆ The opposite of difficult is easy or simple.

dig *verb* (digs, digging, dug)

To dig means to move soil away to make a hole in the ground.

◆ How do you stop a mole digging up the garden?
Hide the spade.

dinner *noun* (dinners)

Dinner is the main meal of the day.

What's for dinner, Mum?

direction *noun* (directions)

1 A direction is the way you go to get somewhere.

The beach is in that direction.

2 Directions are words or pictures that tell you what to do or how to get somewhere.

Can you give me directions to the zoo?

dirt *noun*

Dirt is dust, mud, or earth.

Grace washed the dirt off her hands and face.

a
b
c
d
e
f
g
h
i
j
k
l
m
n
o
p
q
r
s
t
u
v
w
x
y
z

a
b
c
d
e
f
g
h
i
j
k
l
m
n
o
p
q
r
s
t
u
v
w
x
y
z

dirty *adjective* (dirtier, dirtiest)

Something that is dirty is covered with mud, food, or other marks.

How did your clothes get so dirty?

◆ The opposite of dirty is clean.

disappear *verb* (disappears, disappearing, disappeared)

If something disappears, you cannot see it any longer.

After two days, my spots disappeared.

◆ The opposite of disappear is appear.

disappointed *adjective*

If you are disappointed, you feel sad because something you were hoping for did not happen.

Jessica was very disappointed that she couldn't go swimming.

disaster *noun* (disasters)

A disaster is something very bad that happens suddenly.

discover *verb* (discovers, discovering, discovered)

When you discover something, you find out about it or see it for the first time.

I've discovered a secret drawer.

discuss *verb* (discusses, discussing, discussed)

When people discuss things, they talk about them.

We discussed the best way to make a treehouse.

disguise *noun* (disguises)

A disguise is something you wear so that people will not know who you are.

dish *noun* (dishes)

1 A dish is for cooking or serving food.

2 The dishes are all the things that have to be washed up after a meal.

dishwasher *noun* (dishwashers)

A dishwasher is a machine that washes the dishes.

◆ Little words can hide in big words. Can you see the words dish, is, was, wash, as, he, and her hiding in the word dishwasher?

disk *noun* (disks)

A disk is a thin, flat object that you use in a computer to store information.

distance *noun* (distances)

The distance between two places or things is how far they are from each other.

The distance from my house to my school is half a mile.

disturb *verb* (disturbs, disturbing, disturbed)

If you disturb someone, you interrupt what they are doing.

Please don't disturb me when I'm working.

dive *verb* (dives, diving, dived)

When you dive, you jump head first into water.

Serena dived off the top diving board.

◆ Some other words that end with the letters 'ive' are: alive drive five hive

divide *verb* (divides, dividing, divided)

1 If you divide something, you make it into smaller pieces.

Divide the cake into six pieces.

2 When you divide numbers, you find out how many times one goes into another.

Six divided by two is three.

do *verb* (does, doing, did, done)

When you do something, you finish it or spend time on it.

Alex likes to do jigsaws.

doctor *noun* (doctors)

A doctor is someone whose job is to help people who are sick or hurt to get better.

◆ The word doctor comes from a Latin word that means 'teacher'.

does SEE **do**

I like to watch while Grandma does the baking.

dog *noun* (dogs)

A dog is an animal that people keep as a pet or to do work.

◆ A baby dog is called a puppy.

There are many different types of dog. Here are some of them: bloodhound, bulldog, collie, dachshund, Dalmatian, German shepherd, Labrador, poodle, sheepdog, spaniel, terrier.

doing SEE **do**

What are you doing?

doll *noun* (dolls)

A doll is a toy that looks like a baby or a small person.

dolphin *noun* (dolphins)

A dolphin is an animal that lives in the sea. Dolphins are very clever and friendly.

done SEE **do**

Have you done your homework yet?

donkey *noun* (donkeys)

A donkey is an animal that looks like a small horse with long ears.

One of Winnie-the-Pooh's friends is a donkey called Eeyore.

don't

Don't is short for do not.

I don't like spiders.

door *noun* (doors)

A door closes or opens the entrance to something like a house or a room.

a b c **d** e f g h i j k l m n o p q r s t u v w x y z

a
b
c
d
e
f
g
h
i
j
k
l
m
n
o
p
q
r
s
t
u
v
w
x
y
z

down

Down means to a lower place.

The soldiers marched down the hill.

◆ The opposite of down is up.

Some other words that end with the letters 'own' are: brown clown crown frown town

drag *verb* (drags, dragging, dragged)

If you drag something, you pull it along the ground.

dragon *noun* (dragons)

In stories, a dragon is a monster that has wings and can breathe out fire.

◆ The word dragon comes from a Greek word that means 'a snake'.

drain *noun* (drains)

A drain is a pipe that carries away water.

I pulled out the plug in the bath and the water went down the drain.

◆ Some other words that end with the letters 'ain' are: brain chain grain main pain rain train

drank SEE **drink**

I was so thirsty I drank two whole glasses of lemonade.

draw *verb* (draws, drawing, drew, drawn)

When you draw, you make a picture with a pen, pencil, or crayon.

draw *noun* (draws)

If a game ends in a draw, both sides have the same score.

drawer *noun* (drawers)

A drawer is a box for keeping things in that slides in and out of a piece of furniture.

drawing *noun* (drawings)

A drawing is a picture made with a pen, pencil, or crayon.

◆ Little words can hide in big words. Can you see the words draw, raw, win, and wing hiding in the word drawing?

drawn SEE **draw**

I've drawn a funny monster.

dream *verb* (dreams, dreaming, dreamed, dreamt)

When you dream, you see and hear things in your mind while you are asleep.

Last night I dreamed I could fly.

dress *noun* (dresses)

A dress is something that girls and women wear. It is like a skirt and top in one.

dress *verb* (dresses, dressing, dressed)

When you dress, you put your clothes on.

I'll help you dress the baby.

◆ Some other words that end with the letters 'ess' are: chess guess less mess press

drew SEE **draw**

Mina drew a picture of a bird.

drink *verb* (drinks, drinking, drank, drunk)

When you drink, you swallow liquid.
Would you like something to drink?

drink *noun* (drinks)

A drink is a liquid that you swallow.
Would you like a drink of orange juice?

drip *verb* (drips, dripping, dripped)

When liquid drips, it falls in drops.
Rain was dripping through a hole in the roof.

◆ Some other words that end with the letters 'ip' are: chip hip lip ship slip trip

drive *verb* (drives, driving, drove, driven)

When someone drives a car, a truck, or a bus, they make it go where they want.
The man who drives the school bus is called Eddie.

◆ Some other words that end with the letters 'ive' are: alive dive five hive

driven SEE **drive**

My sister has never driven on her own before.

drop *noun* (drops)

A drop is a tiny amount of liquid.
There was a drop of blood from the cut on my finger.

drop *verb* (drops, dropping, dropped)

If you drop something, you let it fall.
I dropped one of the eggs on the floor.

◆ Some other words that end with the letters 'op' are: chop hop shop stop top

drown *verb* (drowns, drowning, drowned)

If someone drowns, they die under water because they cannot breathe.

drum *noun* (drums)

A drum is a musical instrument that you play by hitting it with a stick.

drunk SEE **drink**

I've already drunk my orange juice.

dry (drier, driest)

Something that is dry is not damp or wet.
Your socks are dry enough to put on.

◆ The opposite of dry is wet or damp.

duck *noun* (ducks)

A duck is a bird that lives near water. It has webbed feet for swimming.

◆ A baby duck is called a duckling.

dungeon *noun* (dungeons)

A dungeon is a prison underneath a castle.

dust *noun*

Dust is dry dirt like a powder.

◆ When something is covered in dust, it is dusty.

a b c **d** e f g h i j k l m n o p q r s t u v w x y z

Ee

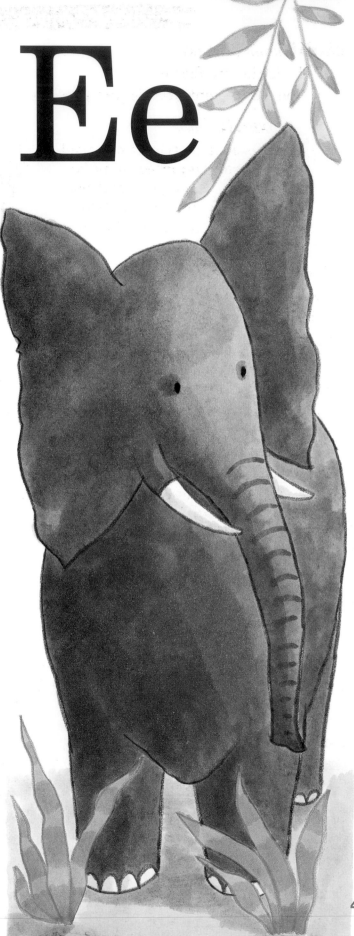

eagle *noun* (eagles)

An eagle is a large bird with a curved beak. Eagles have their nests in high places like mountains.

ear *noun* (ears)

Your ears are the two parts of your body that you use for hearing.

Elephants have very big ears.

early *adjective* (earlier, earliest)

1 Early means near the beginning of something.

The farmer milks the cows in the early morning.

2 If someone is early, they arrive before you expect them.

You're too early — come back later.

◆ The opposite of early is late.

earn *verb* (earns, earning, earned)

If you earn money, you work for it.

earth *noun*

1 The Earth is the planet that we live on.

2 Earth is the soil or dirt that plants grow in.

In the spring, the seeds in the earth begin to grow.

easel *noun* (easels)

An easel is a stand for holding a picture while you are painting it.

east *noun*

East is the direction of the rising sun.

easy *adjective* (easier, easiest)

If something is easy, you can do it or understand it without any trouble.

This game is really easy to play.

◆ The opposite of easy is hard or difficult.

eat *verb* (eats, eating, ate, eaten)
When you eat, you take food into your body.
'Someone's been eating my porridge!',
said Daddy Bear.
◆ Some other words that end with the letters 'eat' are: beat heat meat neat seat wheat

echo *noun* (echoes)
An echo is a sound that you hear again when it bounces back off something solid.
Jake shouted 'Hello!' in the cave and
heard the echo 'Hello!' come back to him.

edge *noun* (edges)
An edge is the part along the end or side of something.
She lived in a cottage at the
edge of the forest.

effect *noun* (effects)
An effect is anything that happens because of something else.
The effect of all the rain
was a flood.

effort *noun* (efforts)
Effort is the hard work you put into something you are trying to do.
Beth made a real effort to write neatly.

egg *noun* (eggs)
Baby birds, reptiles, amphibians, fish, and insects live inside eggs until they are big enough to be born. Birds' eggs are oval, with a thin hard shell.
The magic goose laid a golden egg.
◆ When an egg comes out of the body of a bird, insect, or other animal, we say that the animal lays an egg. When a baby animal comes out of the egg, we say that the egg hatches.

eight *noun* (eights)
Eight is the number 8.
◆ The word eight sounds just like ate.

elastic *noun*
Elastic is a strip of material that can be pulled to make it longer. When you let it go, it goes back to its usual size.
Katie tied her hair back with an
elastic band.

elbow *noun* (elbows)
Your elbow is the bony part in the middle of your arm, where it bends.

electricity *noun*
Electricity is power that moves along wires. It is used to give light and heat, and to make machines work.

elephant *noun* (elephants)
An elephant is a very large, grey animal with a very long nose, called a trunk, big ears, and tusks.
Elephants are the largest
animals on land.
◆ When elephants make a noise, they trumpet.

What do you get if you cross an elephant with a goldfish? Swimming trunks.

eleven *noun* (elevens)
Eleven is the number 11.

empty *adjective* (emptier, emptiest)
Something that is empty has nothing in it.
The treasure chest
was empty.
◆ The opposite of empty is full.

a b c d **e** f g h i j k l m n o p q r s t u v w x y z

end *noun* (ends)

The end is the last part of something.
I read the book right to the end.

end *verb* (ends, ending, ended)

If something ends, it finishes or stops.
What time does the film end?
◆ The opposite of end is begin or start.

enemy *noun* (enemies)

An enemy is a person who wants to hurt or fight you.
◆ The opposite of enemy is friend.

energetic *adjective*

Someone who is energetic moves quickly and does a lot of things.

energy *noun*

1 If you have energy, you can move quickly and do a lot of things.
Mina has lots of energy — she's always running around.

2 Energy is the power to make machines work.

engine *noun* (engines)

An engine is a machine that uses fuel to make things move.
The driver started the engine and the bus moved off.

enjoy *verb* (enjoys, enjoying, enjoyed)

If you enjoy something, you like doing it.
I enjoy playing football with my friends.

enormous *adjective*

Something enormous is very big.

enough

If you have enough of something, you do not need any more.
Have you had enough to eat?

enter *verb* (enters, entering, entered)

If you enter a place, you go into it.
You can enter the school through the side gate.

entrance *noun* (entrances)

The entrance to a place is the way in.

◆ The opposite of entrance is exit.

envelope *noun* (envelopes)

An envelope is a paper cover for a letter.

◆ The word envelope comes from a French word that means 'to wrap up'.

environment *noun* (environments)

The environment is the air, land, and water that surrounds us.

We are learning about protecting the environment.

envy *verb* (envies, envying, envied)

If you envy someone, you wish you could have something they have.

I envy my sister because she has her own bedroom.

equal *verb* (equals, equalling, equalled)

If something equals something else, the two things are the same size or the same number.

Two plus two equals four.

equipment *noun*

Equipment is all the things you need for doing something.

Our school has lots of sports equipment.

escape *verb* (escapes, escaping, escaped)

If a person or animal escapes, they get away from something.

My rabbit keeps escaping from its cage.

a b c d **e** f g h i j k l m n o p q r s t u v w x y z

a b c d **e** f g h i j k l m n o p q r s t u v w x y z

even *adjective*

1 If a number is even, it can be divided by two, with nothing left over.

Two, four, and six are even numbers.

2 If two scores are even, they are the same.

3 If a path is even, it is flat and smooth.

evening *noun* (evenings)

The evening is the time at the end of the day before people go to bed.

every

Every means each person or thing in a group.

Every girl in this room is wearing blue.

everyone *noun*

Everyone means every person.

excellent *adjective*

Excellent means very good.

Hannah is an excellent singer.

excited *adjective*

If you are excited, you are very happy about something and really looking forward to it.

excuse *noun* (excuses)

An excuse is what you say to explain why you have done something so that you will not get into trouble.

You're late again. What's the excuse this time?

exercise *noun* (exercises)

1 Exercise is moving your body to keep fit. *Swimming is good exercise.*

2 An exercise is a piece of work you do to help you learn.

exit *noun* (exits)

An exit is the way out of a place.

◆ The opposite of exit is entrance.

expect *verb* (expects, expecting, expected)

If you expect something, you think it is very likely to happen.

I expect we will lose again.

expensive *adjective*

Something expensive costs a lot of money.

◆ The opposite of expensive is cheap.

explain *verb* (explains, explaining, explained)

If you explain something, you make it clear so that people can understand it.

Can you explain what makes a rainbow appear in the sky?

explode *verb* (explodes, exploding, exploded)

When something explodes, it blows up with a very loud bang.

explore *verb* (explores, exploring, explored)

When you explore, you look carefully round a place for the first time.

The children went off to explore the beach.

extinct *adjective*

If a kind of animal is extinct, there are none living any more.

Dodos have been extinct for over three hundred years.

extra *adjective*

Extra means more than usual.

You should take extra sweaters in case the weather turns cold.

eye *noun* (eyes)

Your eyes are the two parts of your body that you use for seeing.

a b c d **e** f g h i j k l m n o p q r s t u v w x y z

a
b
c
d
e
f
g
h
i
j
k
l
m
n
o
p
q
r
s
t
u
v
w
x
y
z

Ff

face *noun* (faces)

Your face is the front part of your head.

◆ Some other words that end with the letters 'ace' are: lace place race space

factory *noun* (factories)

A factory is a building where people and machines make a large number of things.

fail *verb* (fails, failing, failed)

If someone fails, they try to do something but cannot do it.

The pirates failed to find the treasure and had to leave without it.

fair *adjective* (fairer, fairest)

1 Something that is fair seems right because everyone is treated the same way.

It's not fair! Why does she always sit in the front?

2 Fair can mean light in colour.

The princess had long, fair hair.

fair *noun* (fairs)

Fairs are set up with things like stalls, roundabouts, and other rides so that people can have fun.

◆ Some other words that end with the letters 'air' are: air chair hair pair stair

fairy *noun* (fairies)

In stories, fairies are tiny people who have wings and can do magic.

Tinkerbell is the fairy who teaches Peter Pan how to fly.

fall *verb* (falls, falling, fell, fallen)

When something falls, it comes down suddenly.

Snow was falling from the sky.

◆ Some other words that end with the letters 'all' are: ball call hall tall wall

fallen SEE **fall**

I've fallen over and hurt my knee.

family *noun* (families)

A family is made up of people who are related, especially parents and children.

famous *adjective*

Famous people and things are very well known.

Beatrix Potter is the name of a famous writer.

far (farther, farthest)

Something that is far away is a long way away.

My school is too far to walk to.

◆ Some other words that end with the letters 'ar' are: bar car jar star

farm *noun* (farms)

A farm is a piece of land for growing crops or keeping animals for food.

◆ A person who works on a farm is called a farmer.

fast *adjective* (faster, fastest)

Something that is fast can move quickly.

◆ Another word that means the same as fast is quick.

The opposite of fast is slow.

fasten *verb* (fastens, fastening, fastened)

If you fasten something, you do it up.

You need to fasten your seat belt.

fat *adjective* (fatter, fattest)

A person or animal that is fat has a very thick, round body.

Our cat is getting too fat. Do you think we are feeding him too much?

◆ The opposite of fat is thin.

fat *noun* (fats)

Fat is something like butter or oil that can be used in cooking.

father *noun* (fathers)

A father is a man who has a son or daughter.

fault *noun* (faults)

If something bad is your fault, you made it happen.

It was Karen's fault that the camera wobbled — she made me laugh.

favourite *adjective*

Your favourite is the one you like best.

Winnie-the-Pooh's favourite food is honey.

fear *noun* (fears)

Fear is the feeling you get when you think something bad is going to happen to you.

feast *noun* (feasts)

A feast is a special meal for a lot of people.

feather *noun* (feathers)

A feather is one of the soft, light things that cover a bird and help it to fly.

fed SEE **feed**

We fed the ducks on the pond.

a
b
c
d
e
f
g
h
i
j
k
l
m
n
o
p
q
r
s
t
u
v
w
x
y
z

feed *verb* (feeds, feeding, fed)

If you feed a person or animal, you give them food.

Will you feed the cat, please?

feel *verb* (feels, feeling, felt)

1 If you feel something, you touch it to find out what it is like.

Just feel how soft this kitten is!

2 If you feel a particular way, like excited or tired, that is how you are at the time.

I feel sad now that I'm leaving.

fell SEE **fall**

Humpty Dumpty fell off the wall.

◆ Some other words that end with the letters 'ell' are: bell sell shell spell tell well yell

felt SEE **feel**

After swimming all afternoon I felt very tired.

female *noun* (females)

A female is a person or animal that belongs to the sex that can have babies. Girls and women are female.

◆ The opposite of female is male.

fence *noun* (fences)

A fence is a kind of wall made of wood or wire. People put fences around gardens and fields.

◆ What time is it when an elephant sits on your fence?
Time to get a new fence.

fetch *verb* (fetches, fetching, fetched)

When you fetch something, you go and get it.

few (fewer, fewest)

Few means not many.

I only have a few jelly babies left.

field *noun* (fields)

A field is a piece of land with a fence or hedge around it. Farmers grow crops or grass in fields.

fierce *adjective* (fiercer, fiercest)

A fierce animal looks angry and might attack you.

There was a fierce dog in front of the gate.

fight *verb* (fights, fighting, fought)

When people fight, they try to hurt each other.

'Let's fight till six, and then have dinner,' said Tweedledum to Tweedledee.

◆ Some other words that end with the letters 'ight' are: bright fright light night right tight

fill *verb* (fills, filling, filled)

If you fill something, you put so much into it that you cannot get any more in.

Rose filled her cup to the top.

◆ The opposite of fill is empty.

Some other words that end with the letters 'ill' are: bill hill ill kill pill still till will

film *noun* (films)

1 A film is a strip or roll of thin plastic that you put in a camera when you want to take photographs.

2 A film is also a story told in moving pictures. You watch a film at the cinema or on television.

My favourite film is 'Shrek'.

fin *noun* (fins)

A fin is one of the thin, flat parts that stand out from a fish's body. Fins help fish to swim.

find *verb* (finds, finding, found)

When you find something that has been lost, you get it back.

Ryan found his other sock under the bed.

◆ The opposite of find is lose.

fine *adjective* (finer, finest)

1 Fine threads are very thin.

2 Fine weather is dry and sunny.

3 If you say you are fine, you mean you are well and happy.

fine *noun* (fines)

A fine is money that someone has to pay as a punishment.

If you don't take this book back to the library tomorrow, you will have to pay a fine.

finger *noun* (fingers)

Your fingers are the five long, thin parts at the end of your hand.

finish *verb* (finishes, finishing, finished)

When you finish, you come to the end of something.

Tom was still eating but Holly had finished.

◆ Other words that mean the same as finish are end and complete.

fire *noun* (fires)

1 Fire is the heat, flames, and bright light that comes from something that is burning.

The animals ran away from the fire.

2 A fire is something that keeps people warm.

Grandpa was sitting by the fire.

fire brigade *noun* (fire brigades)

A fire brigade is a group of people called fire fighters. Their job is to put out fires.

fire engine *noun* (fire engines)

A fire engine is a large truck that takes fire fighters, hoses, and ladders to a fire.

firework *noun* (fireworks)

A firework is a paper tube filled with powder. When you light it, the firework makes a loud bang or burns with coloured sparks or flames.

On Bonfire Night we went to the fireworks display in the park.

firm (firmer, firmest)

If something is firm, it is hard or is fixed so that it will not give way.

David tested the old bridge to make sure it was firm before he went across.

◆ Other words that mean the same as firm are hard, solid, and strong.

first

If something is first, it comes before all the others.

The first letter of the alphabet is A.

◆ The opposite of first is last.

a
b
c
d
e
f
g
h
i
j
k
l
m
n
o
p
q
r
s
t
u
v
w
x
y
z

a
b
c
d
e
f
g
h
i
j
k
l
m
n
o
p
q
r
s
t
u
v
w
x
y
z

fish *noun* (fish or fishes)

A fish is an animal that lives and breathes under water. Fish are covered with scales, and they have fins and a tail for swimming.

◆ There are many different types of fish. Here are some of them: carp, cod, eel, goldfish, haddock, halibut, herring, mackerel, perch, pike, pilchard, plaice, salmon, sardine, seahorse, shark, sole, trout.

fish *verb* (fishes, fishing, fished)

If you fish, you try to catch fish.

fit *verb* (fits, fitting, fitted)

If something fits you, it is the right size and shape.

The glass slipper fitted Cinderella perfectly.

fit *adjective* (fitter, fittest)

Someone who is fit is healthy.

fizzy *adjective* (fizzier, fizziest)

A fizzy drink is one that is full of little bubbles. If a drink fizzes, it makes a hissing sound because of all the little bubbles.

◆ Some words sound like the thing they mean. The word fizzy actually sounds like the hissing sound that the bubbles make in a fizzy drink.

flag *noun* (flags)

A flag is a piece of cloth with a pattern on it. It is used as a symbol of a country or a group of people.

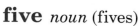

five *noun* (fives)

Five is the number 5.

◆ In this dictionary, the word that comes after five is not six but . . . fix!

Some other words that end with the letters 'ive' are: alive dive drive hive

fix *verb* (fixes, fixing, fixed)

1 If you fix something that is broken, you mend it.

Can you fix my computer?

2 If you fix something somewhere, you join it firmly to something else.

flame *noun* (flames)

A flame is one of the hot, bright strips of light you see rising up from a fire.

◆ Some other words that end with the letters 'ame' are: blame frame game name same tame

flap *verb* (flaps, flapping, flapped)

When a bird flaps its wings, it moves them up and down quickly.

flash *noun* (flashes)

A flash is a sudden bright light.

A flash of lightning lit up the sky.

flat *adjective* (flatter, flattest)

Something that is flat does not slope or have any bumps or wrinkles. The top of a table is flat.

Find something flat to put your paper on.

flat *noun* (flats)

A flat is a home. It is a set of rooms inside a house or big building.

◆ Some other words that end with the letters 'at' are: bat cat hat mat pat rat sat that

flavour *noun* (flavours)

The flavour of food or drink is what it tastes like.

My favourite flavour of ice cream is strawberry.

flew SEE **fly**

A helicopter flew over our heads.

flipper *noun* (flippers)

The flippers on animals such as seals, turtles, or penguins are the flat arms that they use for swimming.

float *verb* (floats, floating, floated)

1 If something floats, it stays on top of a liquid.

2 If something floats through the air, it drifts along gently.

The red balloon floated above the rooftops.

◆ The opposite of float is sink.

Some other words that end with the letters 'oat' are: boat coat goat throat

flock *noun* (flocks)

A flock is a group of birds or sheep.

◆ The word flock comes from an old word that meant 'a crowd of people'.

floor *noun* (floors)

A floor is the part of a room or building that people walk on.

We all sat on the floor watching television.

◆ The part of a room opposite the floor is the ceiling.

flour *noun*

Flour is a powder made from wheat that you use to make bread and cakes.

◆ The word flour sounds just like flower.

flow *verb* (flows, flowing, flowed)

To flow means to move along like water.

The stream flows very fast here.

flower *noun* (flowers)

A flower is the part of a plant that makes seeds. Many flowers are brightly coloured.

◆ The word flower sounds just like flour.

There are many different types of flower. Here are some of them: bluebell, buttercup, carnation, crocus, daffodil, daisy, dandelion, foxglove, pansy, rose, sunflower, tulip

a b c d e **f** g h i j k l m n o p q r s t u v w x y z

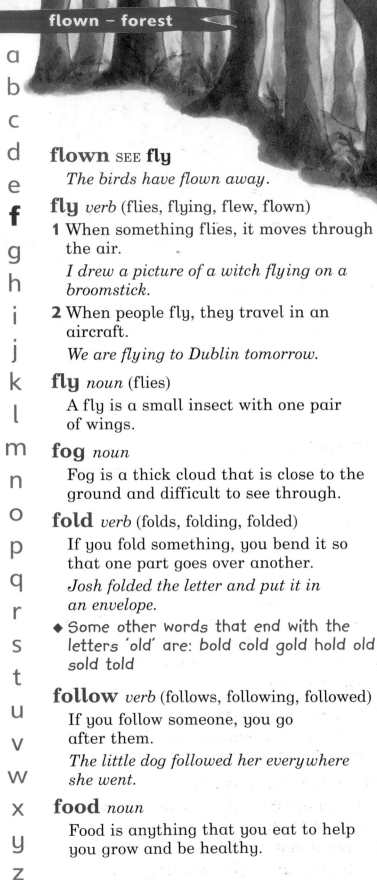

flown SEE **fly**

The birds have flown away.

fly *verb* (flies, flying, flew, flown)

1 When something flies, it moves through the air.

I drew a picture of a witch flying on a broomstick.

2 When people fly, they travel in an aircraft.

We are flying to Dublin tomorrow.

fly *noun* (flies)

A fly is a small insect with one pair of wings.

fog *noun*

Fog is a thick cloud that is close to the ground and difficult to see through.

fold *verb* (folds, folding, folded)

If you fold something, you bend it so that one part goes over another.

Josh folded the letter and put it in an envelope.

◆ Some other words that end with the letters 'old' are: bold cold gold hold old sold told

follow *verb* (follows, following, followed)

If you follow someone, you go after them.

The little dog followed her everywhere she went.

food *noun*

Food is anything that you eat to help you grow and be healthy.

foot *noun* (feet)

Your feet are the parts of your body at the end of your legs that you stand on.

football *noun* (footballs)

1 Football is a game played by two teams who kick a ball and try to score goals.

2 A football is a large ball that you use to play football.

footprint *noun* (footprints)

A footprint is a mark left by a foot or shoe on the ground.

for

This present is for Sophie.

forehead *noun* (foreheads)

Your forehead is the part of your face above your eyes.

foreign *adjective*

Something that is foreign comes from another country.

We've got a foreign car. It was made in Germany.

forest *noun* (forests)

A forest is a place where a lot of trees are growing together.

Snow White was left all alone in the forest.

forever

Forever means always.

forgave SEE forgive

My sister broke my doll, but I forgave her because it was an accident.

forget *verb* (forgets, forgetting, forgot, forgotten)

If you forget something, you do not remember it.

I'm always forgetting my football boots.

◆ The opposite of forget is remember.

forgive *verb* (forgives, forgiving, forgave, forgiven)

If you forgive someone, you stop being angry with them.

Please forgive me for missing your birthday party.

forgiven SEE forgive

I have forgiven you for losing my pen.

forgot SEE forget

I forgot to take my lunch to school, so I was hungry all afternoon.

forgotten SEE forget

I know that boy but I've forgotten his name.

◆ Little words can hide in big words. Can you see the words for, or, go, got, and ten hiding in the word forgotten?

fork *noun* (forks)

A fork is a tool with three or four thin pointed parts. People use small forks for eating and large forks for digging in the garden.

fortnight *noun* (fortnights)

A fortnight is two weeks.

fought SEE fight

The two armies fought each other all day.

found SEE find

I've found my other shoe at last!

four *noun* (fours)

Four is the number 4.

fox *noun* (foxes)

A fox is a wild animal that looks like a dog with a long furry tail.

◆ A female fox is called a vixen. A baby fox is called a cub.

frame *noun* (frames)

A frame is something that fits round the edge of a picture or window.

free *adjective* (freer, freest)

1 If you are free, you can do what you like or go where you like.

2 Free things do not cost anything.
Children under five can get in free.

a b c d e **f** g h i j k l m n o p q r s t u v w x y z

a
b
c
d
e
f
g
h
i
j
k
l
m
n
o
p
q
r
s
t
u
v
w
x
y
z

freeze *verb* (freezes, freezing, froze, frozen)

1 When water freezes, it changes into ice.

2 People freeze food to keep it from going bad.

3 If you say you are freezing, you mean you are very cold.

fresh *adjective* (fresher, freshest)

1 Fresh food has just been picked or made.

I love the smell of fresh bread.

2 Fresh water is not salty.

Some fish live in the sea and some fish live in fresh water, like lakes and rivers.

3 Fresh air is clean and pure.

Friday *noun* (Fridays)

Friday is the sixth day of the week.

fridge *noun* (fridges)
SEE **refrigerator**

friend *noun* (friends)

A friend is someone you know well and like and who likes you too.

Winnie-the-Pooh has friends called Tigger and Eeyore.

◆The opposite of friend is enemy.

friendly *adjective* (friendlier, friendliest)

Someone who is friendly is kind and helpful.

frighten *verb* (frightens, frightening, frightened)

If something frightens a person or animal, it makes them feel afraid.

Fireworks always frighten our dog Razzle.

frog *noun* (frogs)

A frog is a small animal with a smooth, wet skin. Frogs live near water and have strong back legs for jumping.

The princess kissed the frog and he turned into a handsome prince.

◆ A baby frog is called a tadpole. When frogs make a noise, they croak.

from

I've got a postcard from Ali.

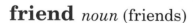

front *noun* (fronts)

The front of anything is the side that people usually see first.

We walked up the path and knocked at the front door.

frown *verb* (frowns, frowning, frowned)

When you frown, you look cross or worried and lines come onto your forehead.

◆ Some other words that end with the letters 'own' are: brown clown crown down town

froze SEE **freeze**

It was so cold that the pond froze.

frozen SEE **freeze**

Children were skating on the frozen pond.

fruit *noun* (fruits)

Fruit is something like an apple, orange, or banana which grows on a bush or tree. Fruits have seeds in them.

◆ There are many different types of fruit. Here are some of them: apple, apricot, banana, blackberry, cherry, grape, grapefruit, lemon, melon, orange, peach, pear, pineapple, plum, raspberry, strawberry.

fry *verb* (fries, frying, fried)

When you fry food, you cook it in hot oil or fat in a pan.

fuel *noun*

Fuel is something that can be burned to make heat or power.

Coal, wood, and oil can be used as fuel.

full *adjective* (fuller, fullest)

If something is full, there is no more room in it.

The chest was full of gold coins.

◆ The opposite of full is empty.

fun *noun*

When you have fun, you enjoy yourself and feel happy.

◆ Some other words that end with the letters 'un' are: bun gun run sun

funny *adjective* (funnier, funniest)

1 If something is funny, it makes you laugh.

Do you know any funny jokes?

2 Something funny seems strange.

What's that funny smell?

fur *noun*

Fur is the thick soft hair that covers some animals.

furniture *noun*

Furniture is all the big things like beds, tables, chairs, and cupboards that you need in a house.

furry *adjective*

A furry animal is covered in thick soft hair.

a b c d e **f** g h i j k l m n o p q r s t u v w x y z

61

Gg

gale *noun* (gales)

A gale is a very strong wind.

game *noun* (games)

A game is something you play that has rules. Football, chess, and hide-and-seek are games.

◆ Some other words that end with the letters 'ame' are: blame flame frame name same tame

gap *noun* (gaps)

A gap is a space between two things. *The dog squeezed through a gap in the fence.*

garage *noun* (garages)

1 A garage is a building where you keep a car.

2 A garage is also a place that sells fuel or repairs cars.

garden *noun* (gardens)

A garden is a piece of ground where people can grow flowers and vegetables. Someone's garden is usually next to their house.

gas *noun* (gases)

A gas is anything like air, that is not solid or liquid. There are lots of different gases. Some gases have strong smells. Some gases burn easily and are used for heating and cooking.

gate *noun* (gates)

A gate is a kind of door in a wall, fence, or hedge. *Pooh and Piglet sat on the gate.*

gave SEE **give**

The prince gave Sleeping Beauty a kiss.

gentle *adjective* (gentler, gentlest)

If you are gentle, you are kind, quiet, and careful.

Be very gentle with the kitten.

geography *noun*

Geography is learning about the Earth, different countries, and the weather.

gerbil *noun* (gerbils)

A gerbil is a small animal with long back legs and very soft fur. Gerbils are often kept as pets.

get *verb* (gets, getting, got)

If you get something, you go to where it is and bring it back.

I'm going to get my skateboard.

ghost *noun* (ghosts)

A ghost is the spirit of a dead person that some people believe they have seen.

giant *noun* (giants)

A giant is a huge person in fairy tales.

The giant chased Jack down the beanstalk.

giraffe *noun* (giraffes)

A giraffe is a very tall animal with a long neck and long, thin legs.

◆ Why do giraffes have such long necks? Because they've got smelly feet.

girl *noun* (girls)

A girl is a female child or young adult.

give *verb* (gives, giving, gave, given)

If you give something to someone, you let them have it.

We are going to give Mum a ride in a hot air balloon for her birthday.

given SEE **give**

I've already given you two biscuits.

glad *adjective* (gladder, gladdest)

If you are glad, you are happy about something.

I'm glad you are coming to stay.

◆ Some other words that end with the letters 'ad' are: bad dad had sad

glass *noun* (glasses)

1 Glass is a hard material that you can see through. It is used to make windows and bottles.

2 A glass is a kind of cup made of glass.

glasses *noun*

People wear glasses in front of their eyes to help them see better. Glasses are two pieces of glass or plastic in a frame.

Jack wore a pair of round, red glasses.

63

a
b
c
d
e
f
g
h
i
j
k
l
m
n
o
p
q
r
s
t
u
v
w
x
y
z

glove *noun* (gloves)

A glove is a covering for the hand with places for the thumb and each finger.

glue *noun*

Glue is a thick liquid used for sticking things together.

go *verb* (goes, going, went, gone)

If you go somewhere, you move from one place to another.

Let's all go to the park.

goal *noun* (goals)

1 A goal is the two posts that a ball must go between to score a point in games like football.

2 A goal is also a point that is scored when a ball goes into the goal.

goat *noun* (goats)

A goat is an animal with horns and sometimes a beard under its chin. Goats are sometimes kept for their milk.

◆ A male goat is called a billy goat. A female goat is called a nanny goat. A baby goat is called a kid.

Some other words that end with the letters 'oat' are: boat coat float throat

going

If you are going to do something, you are about to do it.

gold *noun*

Gold is a valuable yellow metal that can be made into jewellery.

Everything King Midas touched turned to gold.

◆ Some other words that end with the letters 'old' are: bold cold fold hold old sold told

goldfish *noun* (goldfish)

A goldfish is a small orange fish often kept as a pet.

gone SEE **go**

Everyone has gone home.

good *adjective* (better, best)

1 If you say something is good, you like it. *This is a good video.*

2 Work that is good is done well.

3 If you are good, you behave well.

4 A good person is kind and caring.

goodbye

You say goodbye when you leave someone.

goose *noun* (geese)

A goose is a large bird with a long neck that lives near water.

◆ A male goose is called a gander. A baby goose is called a gosling.

gorilla *noun* (gorillas)

A gorilla is a large, strong ape.

got SEE **get**

Amy got her coat from the car.

grain *noun* (grains)

A grain of rice, wheat, or other cereal is a seed from the plant.

◆ Some other words that end with the letters 'ain' are: brain chain drain main pain rain train

grandfather *noun* (grandfathers)

Your grandfather is the father of your father or mother. You can also call him your grandpa.

◆ Little words can hide in big words. Can you *see* the words ran, and, fat, father, at, the, he, and her hiding in the word grandfather?

grandmother *noun* (grandmothers)

Your grandmother is the mother of your father or mother. You can also call her your grandma.

grape *noun* (grapes)

A grape is a small green or purple fruit that grows in bunches.

grass *noun*

Grass is a green plant with thin leaves. There are usually lots of these plants growing close together in gardens and fields.

great *adjective*

1 Great means very good.

We all had a great time at the party.

2 Great also means large.

The giant lived in a great big house.

greedy *adjective* (greedier, greediest)

Someone who is greedy wants more than their fair share of money or food.

green *adjective*

Green is the colour of grass and summer leaves.

grew SEE **grow**

The beanstalk grew right up into the sky.

ground *noun*

The ground is the earth or other surface that you walk on outside.

Under the tree there were lots of apples on the ground.

group *noun* (groups)

A group is a number of people or things that are all together or belong together.

A group of children came out of the park.

grow *verb* (grows, growing, grew, grown)

When somebody or something grows, they get bigger.

'The Jungle Book' is about a boy called Mowgli who grows up in the jungle.

guess *verb* (guesses, guessing, guessed)

When you guess, you give the answer to something without really knowing if it is right.

Can you guess what's in this box?

◆ Some other words that end with the letters 'ess' are: chess dress less mess press

guitar *noun* (guitars)

A guitar is a musical instrument with strings. You play it with your fingers.

a
b
c
d
e
f
g
h
i
j
k
l
m
n
o
p
q
r
s
t
u
v
w
x
y
z

Hh

a
b
c
d
e
f
g
h
i
j
k
l
m
n
o
p
q
r
s
t
u
v
w
x
y
z

had SEE **have**

Amy had a bad cold last week.

◆ Some other words that end with the letters 'ad' are: bad dad glad sad

hair *noun*

Hair is the soft covering that grows on your head and body.

Rapunzel had long, beautiful hair.

◆ Some other words that end with the letters 'air' are: air chair fair pair stair

half *noun* (halves)

A half is one of two equal parts.

Let's cut the pizza in half.

hamster *noun* (hamsters)

A hamster is a small furry animal, with places inside its cheeks where it can hold food. Hamsters are often kept as pets.

Put the hamster back in its cage.

hand *noun* (hands)

Your hands are the parts of your body that you use for holding things. A hand has four fingers and a thumb.

◆ Some other words that end with the letters 'and' are: band land sand stand

handle *noun* (handles)

A handle is the part of something that you use to hold or carry it. Cups, baskets, pots, and doors have handles.

hang *verb* (hangs, hanging, hung)

When you hang something, you fix the top of it to a hook or nail.

Please hang your coat up.

happy *adjective* (happier, happiest)

When you are happy, you feel pleased about something.

Tigger was happy to see his friends.

◆ Other words that mean the same as happy are glad and pleased.

The opposite of happy is sad.

hard *adjective* (harder, hardest)

1 Something that is hard is not soft.

This bed is too hard!

2 Something that is hard to do is not easy.

This sum is too hard!

has SEE **have**

Katie has three teddies.

hat *noun* (hats)

A hat is something you wear on your head.

◆ Some other words that end with the letters 'at' are: bat cat flat mat pat rat sat that

hatch *verb* (hatches, hatching, hatched)

When a baby bird hatches, it breaks out of its egg.

hate *verb* (hates, hating, hated)

If you hate someone or something, you feel very strongly that you do not like them or it.

I hate getting up when it is still dark.

have *verb* (has, having, had)

If you have something, it is with you or you own or feel it.

I have a new bike.

I have a headache.

having SEE **have**

We are having a picnic tomorrow.

hay *noun*

Hay is dry grass that is used to feed animals.

◆ Some other words that end with the letters 'ay' are: day lay may pay play ray say stay way

he

Stephen says he is hungry.

head *noun* (heads)

1 Your head is the part of your body that is above your neck and has your brain in it.

2 The head of something like a school is the person in charge.

Our school has a new head teacher.

healthy *adjective* (healthier, healthiest)

1 If you feel healthy, you feel well and full of energy.

Eating the right food helps you to stay healthy.

2 Healthy things are good for you.

Wholewheat bread is very healthy.

hear *verb* (hears, hearing, heard)

When you hear, you take in sounds through your ears.

Can you hear that dog barking?

◆ The word hear sounds just like here.

heart *noun* (hearts)

Your heart is a part of your body inside your chest. It pumps blood around your body.

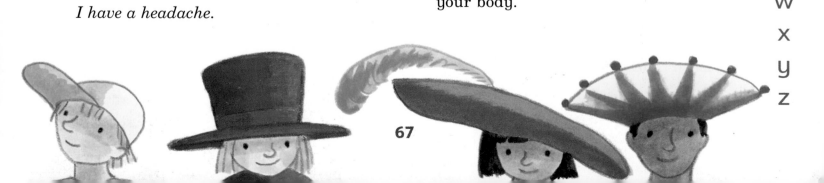

a
b
c
d
e
f
g
h
i
j
k
l
m
n
o
p
q
r
s
t
u
v
w
x
y
z

heavy *adjective* (heavier, heaviest)
Something that is heavy is hard to lift or carry because it weighs a lot.
◆ The opposite of heavy is light.

hedge *noun* (hedges)
A hedge is a kind of wall made by bushes growing close together.

held SEE **hold**
Mum held my hand tightly.

helicopter *noun* (helicopters)
A helicopter is a small aircraft without wings. It has large blades that spin round on top. It can fly straight up from the ground and hover in the air.

help *verb* (helps, helping, helped)
When you help somebody, you do something useful for them.
Can you help me with my homework?

hen *noun* (hens)
A hen is a female chicken.

her
Megan is brushing her hair.
Shareem is my best friend. I like her very much.

here
Here means in this place.
I'll meet you here in ten minutes.
◆ The word here sounds just like hear.

hid SEE **hide**
Josh and Katie hid behind the boulder.

hidden SEE **hide**
Sophie has hidden my shoes and I can't find them.

hide *verb* (hides, hiding, hid, hidden)
1 When you hide, you get into a place where no one can see you.
2 If you hide something, you put it into a place where no one can see it.
◆ Some other words that end with the letters 'ide' are: bride pride ride side tide wide

high *adjective* (higher, highest)
1 Something like a wall or a mountain that is high goes up a long way.
2 If something is high in the air, it is a long way up.
I threw a ball high into the air.
◆ The opposite of high is low.

hill *noun* (hills)
A hill is land that is higher than the land around it. Hills are smaller than mountains.
Jack and Jill went up the hill.
◆ Some other words that end with the letters 'ill' are: bill fill ill kill pill still till will

him
This is my dog.
I call him Razzle.

hippopotamus *noun*
(hippopotamuses or hippopotami)

A hippopotamus is a large animal with a large head and short legs. It lives near rivers and lakes in Africa.

◆ A hippopotamus is called a hippo for short.

The word hippopotamus comes from a Greek word that means 'a river horse'.

69

a
b
c
d
e
f
g
h
i
j
k
l
m
n
o
p
q
r
s
t
u
v
w
x
y
z

his

Jason is holding his puppy.

history *noun*

History is learning about what happened in the past.

hit *verb* (hits, hitting, hit)

If you hit something, you touch it hard.
I hit the ball over the fence.

hive *noun* (hives)

A hive is a kind of box for keeping bees in.

◆ Some other words that end with the letters 'ive' are: alive dive drive five

hold *verb* (holds, holding, held)

1 If you hold something, you have it in your hands or arms.
Can I hold the rabbit?

2 To hold means to have room inside for something.
This case will hold all my pencils.

◆ Some other words that end with the letters 'old' are: bold cold fold gold old sold told

hole *noun* (holes)

A hole is a gap or opening in something.
There's a hole in my sock.

◆ The word hole sounds just like whole.

holiday *noun* (holidays)

A holiday is time off from school or work.

hollow *adjective*

Something hollow has an empty space inside it.
The magpie hid the gold ring in the hollow tree.

◆ The opposite of hollow is solid.

home *noun* (homes)

A person's home is the place where they live.

honey *noun*

Honey is a sweet, sticky food made by bees.
Pooh was in his house, counting his pots of honey.

hoof *noun* (hoofs or hooves)

A hoof is the hard part of a horse's foot. Cows and deer have hoofs, too.

hop *verb* (hops, hopping, hopped)

When you hop, you jump on one leg. Some animals and birds hop on two legs together.

◆ Some other words that end with the letters 'op' are: chop drop shop stop top

hope *verb* (hopes, hoping, hoped)

When you hope that something is going to happen, you want it to happen.
I hope you get better soon.

horn *noun* (horns)

A horn is a kind of pointed bone that grows out of the heads of cows and other animals.

horse *noun* (horses)

A horse is an animal with hoofs that is used for riding and pulling carts.

◆ A male horse is called a stallion. A female horse is called a mare. A baby horse is called a foal. The long hair on a horse's neck is called a mane.

hospital *noun* (hospitals)

A hospital is a place where people who are ill or hurt are looked after.

hot *adjective* (hotter, hottest)

1 When something is hot, it burns if you touch it.

Don't touch the iron — it's hot.

2 If you feel hot, you are too warm.

◆ The opposite of hot is cold.

house *noun* (houses)

A house is a building where people live.

hover *verb* (hovers, hovering, hovered)

If something hovers, it stays in one place in the air.

how

How do you make chocolate brownies?

hug *verb* (hugs, hugging, hugged)

If you hug someone, you put your arms around them and hold them tightly.

huge *adjective*

Something huge is very big.

There was a huge dragon in the cave.

human *noun* (humans)

A human is a man, woman, or child.

hump *noun* (humps)

A hump is a big lump on a camel's back.

hung SEE **hang**

Yasmin hung her coat on the hook.

hungry *adjective* (hungrier, hungriest)

If you are hungry, you want something to eat.

hunt *verb* (hunts, hunting, hunted)

1 To hunt means to go after a wild animal to kill it.

Owls hunt at night.

2 When you hunt for something, you look carefully for it.

I've hunted everywhere for my pen.

hurry *verb* (hurries, hurrying, hurried)

When you hurry, you move or do something quickly.

Let's hurry or we'll be late.

hurt *verb* (hurts, hurting, hurt)

When something hurts, you feel pain there.

This scratch really hurts.

hutch *noun* (hutches)

A hutch is a kind of cage for a pet rabbit.

a b c d e f g **h** i j k l m n o p q r s t u v w x y z

71

a b c d e f g h **i** j k l m n o p q r s t u v w x y z

Ii

ice *noun*

Ice is water that has frozen hard.

◆ Some other words that end with the letters 'ice' are: dice mice nice price rice

ice cream *noun* (ice creams)

Ice cream is a sweet, frozen food made from milk or cream.

I scream, you scream, we all scream for ice cream.

icicle *noun* (icicles)

An icicle is a hanging piece of ice made from dripping water that has frozen hard.

There is an icicle on my tricycle!

idea *noun* (ideas)

An idea is something that you have thought of.

I've got a great idea for a story.

if

Let me know if you can come to my party.

igloo *noun* (igloos)

An igloo is a house made from blocks of hard snow or ice.

iguana *noun* (iguanas)

An iguana is a large lizard that lives in trees in hot countries.

ill *adjective*

Someone who is ill does not feel well.

◆ Some other words that end with the letters 'ill' are: bill fill hill kill pill still till will

illness *noun* (illnesses)

Illness is when you do not feel well.

I missed school for a week because of illness.

72

imagine *verb* (imagines, imagining, imagined)

If you imagine something, you make a picture of it in your mind.

Imagine you can jump over an igloo.

immediately

If you do something immediately, you do it at once.

Stop all that noise immediately!

important *adjective*

1 If something is important, it matters a lot or is worth thinking about.

It is important to brush your teeth every day.

2 If someone is important, people take a lot of notice of what that person says and does.

impossible *adjective*

If something is impossible, it cannot be done.

It is impossible to jump over a house.

in

The mugs are in the cupboard.

information *noun*

Information is facts that tell people about something.

I need some information about dolphins and whales.

ink *noun*

Ink is the coloured liquid that is used for writing with a pen.

a b c d e f g h **i** j k l m n o p q r s t u v w x y z

insect *noun* (insects)

An insect is a very small creature with six legs. Flies, ants, butterflies, and bees are all insects.

◆ There are many different types of insect. Here are some of them: ant, *bee*, beetle, butterfly, cricket, dragonfly, fly, grasshopper, ladybird, wasp

inside

Look inside the box.

instructions *noun*

Instructions are words and pictures that tell people what to do.

There are instructions for playing the game on the lid of the box.

instrument *noun* (instruments)

1 Instruments are things that help you do a special job.

My dentist has a lot of instruments.

2 An instrument is also something that you can use to make music.

◆ There are many different types of musical instrument. Here are some of them: clarinet, drum, flute, guitar, harp, piano, recorder, tambourine, triangle, trumpet, violin

interesting *adjective*

If something is interesting, you want to spend time on it or want to learn more about it.

I'm reading a very interesting book.

◆ The opposite of interesting is boring.

74

a b c d e f g h **i** j k l m n o p q r s t u v w x y z

interrupt *verb* (interrupts, interrupting, interrupted)

If you interrupt somebody, you stop them in the middle of what they are saying or doing.

Please don't interrupt me when I'm talking.

into

The frog jumped into the pond.

invent *verb* (invents, inventing, invented)

If you invent something new, you are the first person who thinks of how to make it.

Professor Popkiss is always inventing funny machines that go wrong.

◆ A person who invents something is called an inventor.

invisible *adjective*

Things that are invisible cannot be seen.

Harry's cloak has the power to make him invisible.

invite *verb* (invites, inviting, invited)

If you invite someone to a party, you ask them to come to it.

◆ The card that you send to someone when you invite them is an invitation.

iron *noun* (irons)

1 Iron is a strong, heavy metal.
2 An iron is a hot tool that you use to make clothes smooth and flat.

is

My name is Cinderella.

island *noun* (islands)

An island is a piece of land with water all round it.

◆ Why is an island like the letter T? Because it's in the middle of water.

it

Throw the ball in the air and then catch it.

a
b
c
d
e
f
g
h
i
j
k
l
m
n
o
p
q
r
s
t
u
v
w
x
y
z

Jj

jacket *noun* (jackets)

A jacket is a short coat.

jaguar *noun* (jaguars)

A jaguar is a big wild cat with spots on its coat.

jam *noun* (jams)

1 Jam is a food that is made by boiling fruit with sugar until it is thick.

2 A jam is a lot of cars crowded together so that nothing can move.

We've been stuck in a traffic jam for nearly an hour.

jam *verb* (jams, jamming, jammed)

If something jams, it becomes stuck and difficult to move.

This drawer has jammed and won't open.

jar *noun* (jars)

Jars are usually made of glass. They hold things like jam.

◆ Some other words that end with the letters 'ar' are: bar car far star

jelly *noun* (jellies)

Jelly is a sweet, slippery food that shakes when you move it.

jet *noun* (jets)

A jet is a very fast aeroplane.

jewel *noun* (jewels)

A jewel is a valuable and beautiful stone.

The treasure chest was full of jewels.

◆ There are many different types of jewel. Here are some of them: diamond, emerald, pearl, ruby. Things like rings, necklaces, and earrings are called jewellery.

76

jigsaw *noun* (jigsaws)

A jigsaw is a puzzle made from a picture cut into pieces. When you fit the pieces together properly, you can see the picture.

job *noun* (jobs)

1 Someone's job is the work that they do to earn money.

2 A job is also something you have to do.

My job is to take the dog for a walk.

join *verb* (joins, joining, joined)

If you join two things, you put them together.

Join the dots to make a picture.

joint *noun* (joints)

A joint is the place where two parts fit together. Your ankle is the joint between your foot and your leg.

joke *noun* (jokes)

A joke is a short story or a riddle that makes people laugh.

journey *noun* (journeys)

A journey is the travelling that people do to get from one place to another.

The journey takes two hours by bus.

◆ A drive is a journey by car. A flight is a journey by aeroplane. A ride is a journey on a horse or bicycle. A voyage is a journey by ship. An expedition is a journey made to do something.

jug *noun* (jugs)

A jug is used for holding and pouring liquids. It has a handle and a spout.

juice *noun* (juices)

Juice is the liquid that comes out of fruit.

jump *verb* (jumps, jumping, jumped)

When you jump, you go suddenly into the air with both feet off the ground.

The cow jumped over the moon.

◆ Some other words that end with the letters 'ump' are: bump hump lump plump pump thump

jumper *noun* (jumpers)

A jumper is a piece of clothing with long sleeves that you wear on the top part of your body.

jungle *noun* (jungles)

A jungle is a thick forest in a warm, wet part of the world.

Mowgli ran through the jungle.

just

I just got here a minute ago.

Kk

kangaroo *noun* (kangaroos)
A kangaroo is a large, Australian animal with strong back legs that it uses for jumping. A female kangaroo has a pocket at the front, where it carries its baby.

keep *verb* (keeps, keeping, kept)
1 If you keep something, you have it as your own and do not give it away.
Do you want to keep your old teddy?
2 If you keep an animal, you take care of it.
My grandma keeps chickens.
3 To keep also means to make something stay as it is.
Elliot blew on his hands to keep them warm.
◆ Some other words that end with the letters 'eep' are: deep sheep sleep steep

kennel *noun* (kennels)
A kennel is a little house for a dog to sleep in.

kept SEE **keep**
I have kept all my old toys.
When I was small we kept hens.
The dog's barking kept us awake all night.

kettle *noun* (kettles)
A kettle is used to boil water in. It has a handle and a spout.

key *noun* (keys)
1 A key is a piece of metal shaped so that it fits into a lock.
2 A key is also a small bar or button that you press with your finger. Pianos and computers have keys.
◆ The keyboard on a piano or computer is where all the keys are.

78

kick *verb* (kicks, kicking, kicked)

When you kick, you hit something with your foot.

◆ Some other words that end with the letters 'ick' are: brick chick click flick lick pick quick sick stick thick trick

kid *noun* (kids)

1 Kids are children.

2 A kid is also the name for a baby goat.

kill *verb* (kills, killing, killed)

To kill means to make someone or something die.

◆ Some other words that end with the letters 'ill' are: bill fill hill ill pill still till will

kind *adjective* (kinder, kindest)

Someone who is kind is ready to help other people.

It was very kind of you to let us play in your garden.

kind *noun* (kinds)

If things are of the same kind, they belong to the same group.

A collie is a kind of dog.

king *noun* (kings)

A king is a man who has been born to rule a country.

◆ The country that a king or queen rules is called a kingdom.

Some other words that end with the letters 'ing' are: bring ring sing sting string swing thing wing

kiss *verb* (kisses, kissing, kissed)

When you kiss someone, you touch them with your lips.

Georgie Porgie, pudding and pie, kissed the girls and made them cry.

kitchen *noun* (kitchens)

A kitchen is a room where food is cooked.

a b c d e f g h i j **k** l m n o p q r s t u v w x y z

a
b
c
d
e
f
g
h
i
j
k
l
m
n
o
p
q
r
s
t
u
v
w
x
y
z

kite *noun* (kites)

A kite is a light toy that you can fly in the wind at the end of a long piece of string.

◆ Some other words that end with the letters 'ite' are: bite white write

kitten *noun* (kittens)

A kitten is a very young cat.

knee *noun* (knees)

Your knee is the bony part in the middle of your leg where it bends.

◆ When we say words that begin kn, we do not say the k. The letter k is silent.

kneel *verb* (kneels, kneeling, knelt)

When you kneel, you get down on your knees.

knelt SEE **kneel**

Steven knelt down to play with the cat.

knew SEE **know**

I knew the answer to the riddle.
I knew the man Dad was talking to.

knickers *noun*

Knickers are underpants worn by women and girls.

knife *noun* (knives)

A knife is a tool with a long, sharp edge for cutting things.

knight *noun*

A long time ago, a knight was a soldier who wore a suit of armour and fought for a king or queen.

◆ The word knight sounds just like night.

knit *verb* (knits, knitting, knitted)

When people knit, they use wool and a pair of long needles to make clothes.

knock *verb* (knocks, knocking, knocked)

When you knock something, you hit it hard.

I knocked my head on the shelf.
The cat knocked over the vase.
Someone is knocking on the door.

80

a b c d e f g h i j **k** l m n o p q r s t u v w x y z

knot *noun* (knots)

A knot is the twisted part where two pieces of string or rope have been been tied together.

There is a knot in my shoelace.

◆ The word knot sounds just like not.

know *verb* (knows, knowing, knew, known)

1 When you know something, you have found it out and you have it in your mind.

I know the answer to that question.

2 If you know somebody, you have met them before.

I know that boy. He lives on our street.

known SEE **know**

My brother has known how to play chess for two years.

I've known Ahmed for ages.

81

Ll

label *noun* (labels)

A label tells you something about the thing that it is fixed on to. Labels on clothes tell you what they are made of, and how to clean them.

lace *noun* (laces)

1 Lace is a material with a pattern of small holes in it. It is often used to decorate things.

2 A lace is a piece of thin cord that is used to tie up a shoe.

◆ Some other words that end with the letters 'ace' are: face place race space

ladder *noun* (ladders)

A ladder is two long bars with short bars between them. People use ladders for climbing up and down.

lady *noun* (ladies)

Lady is a polite word for a woman.

ladybird *noun* (ladybirds)

A ladybird is a small flying beetle. Most ladybirds are red with black spots.
Ladybird, ladybird, fly away home.

laid SEE **lay**

The magic goose laid a golden egg.

lain SEE **lie**

Alex has lain in bed all day.

lake *noun* (lakes)

A lake is a lot of water with land all round it.

lamb *noun* (lambs)

A lamb is a young sheep.

Mary had a little lamb, its fleece was white as snow.

◆ When we say the word lamb, we do not say the letter b at the end. The letter b is silent. Other words with a silent b at the end are climb and thumb.

lamp *noun* (lamps)

A lamp gives light where you want it.

When Aladdin rubbed the magic lamp, the genie appeared.

land *noun*

Land is all the parts of the earth's surface that are not covered with water.

land *verb* (lands, landing, landed)

When people land, they arrive by aeroplane or boat.

◆ Some other words that end with the letters 'and' are: band hand sand stand

lane *noun* (lanes)

1 A lane is a narrow country road.
2 Wide roads are also divided up into strips called lanes.

language *noun* (languages)

Language is the words that people use to speak or write to each other. There are many different languages spoken in the world.

This dictionary is written in the English language.

◆ The word language comes from a Latin word that means 'tongue'.

lap *noun* (laps)

When you are sitting down, your lap is the part from the top of your legs to your knees.

The cat was curled up on Emma's lap.

lap *verb* (laps, lapping, lapped)

When an animal laps, it drinks using its tongue.

Our kitten lapped up the milk from the bowl.

large *adjective* (larger, largest)

If a thing is large, it is bigger than other things.

Can I have a large bag of popcorn?

◆ Other words that mean the same as large are big, enormous, and huge.

last

If something is last, it comes after all the others.

The last letter of the alphabet is Z.

◆ The opposite of last is first.

a
b
c
d
e
f
g
h
i
j
k
l
m
n
o
p
q
r
s
t
u
v
w
x
y
z

a b c d e f g h i j k **l** m n o p q r s t u v w x y z

late *adjective*
(later, latest)

1 If you are late, you arrive after the proper time.
Sorry I'm late. I missed the bus.

2 Late also means near the end of a time.
These flowers will come up in late spring.

◆ The opposite of late is early.

Some other words that end with the letters 'ate' are: date gate hate plate

laugh *verb* (laughs, laughing, laughed)
When you laugh, you make sounds showing that you are happy or think something is funny.

law *noun* (laws)
A law is a rule that everyone in a country must keep.

lawn *noun* (lawns)
A lawn is the part of a garden that is covered with short grass.

lay *verb*
(lays, laying, laid)

1 If you lay something down, you put it down carefully.
Please lay the towels down on the bed.

2 When you lay a table, you get it ready for a meal.

3 When a bird lays an egg, the egg comes out of the bird's body.
Our hen laid an egg this morning.

◆ Some other words that end with the letters 'ay' are: day hay may pay play ray say stay way

lay SEE **lie** *verb*
We lay on the grass, looking up at the clouds.

layer *noun* (layers)
A layer is something flat that lies over or under another surface.
The front path was covered with a layer of snow.

lazy *adjective* (lazier, laziest)
Lazy people do not like working.

◆ Why is the letter E lazy? Because it's always in bed.

lead *verb* (leads, leading, led)

1 If you lead people, you go in front of them to show them where to go or what to do.

2 If you are leading in a race or game, you are winning it.

3 To lead also means to be in charge of a group.
William, you can lead this team.

◆ This word rhymes with seed.

lead *noun* (leads)
A lead is a strap fixed to a dog's collar so that you can control it.

◆ This word rhymes with seed.

lead *noun*
Lead is a soft, grey metal that is very heavy.

◆ This word rhymes with bed.

leader *noun* (leaders)
A leader is a person or animal that is in charge of a group.

leaf *noun* (leaves)

A leaf is one of the flat parts that grow on plants and trees. Most leaves are green.

learn *verb* (learns, learning, learned, learnt)

When you learn, you get to know something you did not know before.

I am taking lessons to learn how to play the piano.

◆ The opposite of learn is teach.

leather *noun*

Leather is a strong material made from the skins of animals. It is used to make things like bags, gloves, and shoes.

leave *verb* (leaves, leaving, left)

1 If you leave, you go away from a place.
What time do you leave school?

2 If you leave something somewhere, you let it stay where it is.
You can leave your bag here.

led SEE **lead** *verb*

A woman led us through all the rooms in the castle.

Kim led the race from beginning to end.

Sarah led our team on sports day.

left *noun*

Left is the side that is opposite to the right.

◆ The opposite of left is right.

left *verb* SEE **leave**

We left home early in the morning.

I left my coat on the bus.

leg *noun* (legs)

1 Legs are the parts of the body that a person or animal uses for walking.

2 The legs of a table or chair are the parts that touch the floor.

lemon *noun* (lemons)

A lemon is a yellow fruit with a sour taste.

◆ If you mix up all the letters in the word lemon, you can make the name of another fruit — melon.

lend *verb* (lends, lending, lent)

When somebody lends you something, they let you have it for a short time and you promise to give it back later.

Please could you lend me your red pen?

◆ The opposite of lend is borrow.

length *noun* (lengths)

The length of something is how long it is.

How would you measure the length of a giraffe's neck?

lens *noun* (lenses)

A lens is a piece of glass or plastic that makes things look larger or smaller. Lenses are used in things like glasses and cameras.

a b c d e f g h i j k **l** m n o p q r s t u v w x y z

leopard *noun* (leopards)

A leopard is a big wild cat with spots on its coat.

◆ Why couldn't the leopard escape from the zoo?
Because he was always spotted.

less

Less means not as much.

There is less water in a pond than a lake.

◆ The opposite of less is more.

Some other words that end with the letters 'ess' are: chess dress guess mess press

lesson *noun* (lessons)

A lesson is the time when someone is teaching you something.

My brother has piano lessons.

let *verb* (lets, letting, let)

If someone lets you do something, they say you may do it.

Please let me go on the computer.

letter *noun* (letters)

1 A letter is one of the signs used for writing words. A, b, c, and d are letters. There are 26 letters in the alphabet.

2 A letter is also a message that you write to someone.

lever *noun* (levers)

A lever is a bar that you pull down to lift or open something, or to make a machine work.

library *noun* (libraries)

A library is a place where a lot of books are kept. You can go to read them there or borrow them to read at home.

◆ The word library comes from a Latin word that means 'a book'.

lick *verb* (licks, licking, licked)

When you lick something, you move your tongue over it.

◆ The leopard was licking its paws.

Some other words that end with the letters 'ick' are: brick chick click flick kick pick quick sick stick thick trick

lid *noun* (lids)

A lid is a top or cover for something like a box or a jar.

Did you put the lid back on the peanut butter jar?

lie *noun* (lies)

A lie is something you say that you know is not true.

Whenever Pinocchio told a lie, his nose grew longer.

lie *verb* (lies, lying, lay, lain)

If you lie, you rest with your body flat.

'Somebody's been lying in my bed — and here she is!' said Baby Bear.

lifeboat *noun* (lifeboats)

A lifeboat is a boat that goes out to sea to rescue people who are in danger.

lift *verb* (lifts, lifting, lifted)

If you lift something, you pick it up and move it upwards.

This bag is too heavy to lift.

light *noun* (lights)

Light is what lets you see. It comes from the sun, flames, and lamps.

◆ Some other words that end with the letters 'ight' are: bright fight fright night right tight

light *verb* (lights, lighting, lit)

If you light something, you start it burning.

Dad is going to light the fire.

light *adjective* (lighter, lightest)

1 Things that are light are easy to lift or carry.

Feathers are very light.

2 Colours that are light are pale.

I have some light blue jeans.

◆ The opposite of the first meaning of the adjective light is heavy. The opposite of the second meaning of the adjective light is dark.

lightning *noun*

Lightning is the bright light that flashes in the sky when there is a thunderstorm.

like

Something that is like something else is nearly the same.

Max was crying like a baby.

That girl has a hat like mine.

like *verb* (likes, liking, liked)

If you like somebody or something, you think they are nice.

I like cats very much.

likely *adjective*

If something is likely, you expect it to happen.

Do you think it's likely to rain?

line *noun* (lines)

1 A line is a long, thin mark.

Write your name on the line.

2 A line is also a row of people or things.

There was a long line of ants on the ground.

3 A railway line is the set of metal rails that a train moves on.

a b c d e f g h i j k **l** m n o p q r s t u v w x y z

a b c d e f g h i j k **l** m n o p q r s t u v w x y z

lion *noun* (lions)

A lion is a large wild cat. A male lion has a circle of long fur around its head.

◆ A female lion is called a lioness. A baby lion is called a cub. A group of lions is called a pride. When lions make a noise, they roar.

lip *noun* (lips)

Your lips are the outside edges of your mouth.

◆ Some other words that end with the letters 'ip' are: chip drip hip ship slip trip

liquid *noun* (liquids)

A liquid is anything that pours easily, like water, milk, or oil.

list *noun* (lists)

A list is a group of things or names that you write down one after the other. *We need to make a shopping list.*

listen *verb* (listens, listening, listened)

When you listen, you pay attention so that you can hear something. *Kelly's in her bedroom, listening to a CD.*

◆ If you mix up all the letters in the word listen, you can make the word silent.

lit SEE **light** *verb*

It was cold, so we lit the fire.

88

litter *noun* (litters)

1 Litter is paper, empty wrappers, bottles, and other rubbish that people drop or leave behind.

Please take your litter home with you.

2 A litter is all the young animals born to the same mother at the same time.

Our cat had a litter of five kittens.

little *adjective* (littler, littlest)

1 If something is little, it is smaller than other things like it.

In the basket was a little puppy.

2 A little period of time does not last very long.

We'll be home in a little while.

3 A little means not very much.

There's only a little juice left.

◆ The opposite of little is big.

live *verb* (lives, living, lived)

1 If something is living, it is alive.

2 If you live in a place, that is where your home is.

lizard *noun* (lizards)

A lizard is a reptile with a long body, four legs, and a long tail.

load *noun* (loads)

A load is a lot of heavy things to carry.

The truck was carrying a load of rocks.

lock *noun* (locks)

A lock is used to keep things like doors or cases shut. You cannot open a lock without the right key.

lolly *noun* (lollies)

A lolly is a hard sweet on a stick or a piece of fruity ice on a stick.

long *adjective* (longer, longest)

1 Something that is long measures a lot from one end to the other.

Monkey was writing a long list.

2 Something that is long takes a lot of time.

This is a very long film.

◆ The opposite of long is short.

a b c d e f g h i j k **l** m n o p q r s t u v w x y z

look *verb* (looks, looking, looked)

1 When you look, you use your eyes.

Look at the fire engine.

2 If you look for something, you try to find it.

I've looked everywhere for my gloves.

◆ Some other words that end with the letters 'ook' are: book cook hook took

loose *adjective* (looser, loosest)

If something is loose, it is not fixed firmly.

One of these wheels is loose.

Vicky has a loose tooth.

◆ The opposite of loose is tight.

lorry *noun* (lorries)

A lorry is a big, open truck for taking heavy things by road.

◆ See how many times you can say this rhyme quickly: 'Red lorry, yellow lorry — red lorry, yellow lorry'.

lose *verb* (loses, losing, lost)

1 If you lose something, you cannot find it.

I keep losing my pen.

2 If you lose in a game or race, someone beats you.

◆ The opposite of the first meaning of lose is find. The opposite of the second meaning of lose is win.

lost SEE **lose**

Bo Peep lost her sheep.

We lost the game last Saturday.

lost *adjective*

If you are lost, you do not know where you are.

Hansel and Gretel were lost in the wood.

lot *noun* (lots)

A lot is a large number or amount.

There are a lot of shells on this beach.

Robbie has lots of toy cars.

loud *adjective* (louder, loudest)
Something loud is easy to hear.
◆ A word that means the same as loud is noisy.
The opposite of loud is quiet.

love *verb* (loves, loving, loved)
If you love someone, you like them very much.

lovely *adjective* (lovelier, loveliest)
Something lovely is enjoyable or beautiful.
Tigger, Pooh, and Piglet had a lovely day.

low *adjective* (lower, lowest)
If something is low, it is close to the ground.
◆ The opposite of low is high.

loyal *adjective*
If someone is loyal, they always help their friends and don't let them down.

lucky *adjective* (luckier, luckiest)
If someone is lucky, good things seem to happen to them.

lunch *noun* (lunches)
Lunch is the meal that people eat in the middle of the day.

lying SEE **lie** *verb*
That dog has been lying in front of the fire all day.

91

Mm

machine *noun* (machines)

A machine has parts that work together to do a job. Many machines use electricity to make them work.

made SEE make

The Queen of Hearts made some tarts.
The loud bang made us all jump.

magazine *noun* (magazines)

A magazine is a kind of thin book that comes out every week or month. It has stories and pictures in it.

magic *noun*

1 In stories, people use magic to do impossible things.

The wizard turned the little dog into a huge dragon by magic.

2 Magic is also doing clever tricks that seem to be impossible.

I got a magic set for my birthday.

magnet *noun* (magnets)

A magnet is a piece of metal that can make pieces of iron or steel stick to it.

We have magnets in the shape of fruit on our fridge door.

main *adjective*

Main means the most important or the biggest.

We have our main meal of the day in the evening.

◆ Some other words that end with the letters 'ain' are: brain chain drain grain pain rain train

make *verb* (makes, making, made)

1 If you make something, you get something new by putting other things together.

Mum said she'd help me make a cake.

2 If you make a thing happen, it happens because of something you have said or done.

Uncle Bernie's jokes always make us laugh.

◆ Some other words that end with the letters 'ake' are: bake cake lake take

male *noun* (males)

A male is any person or animal that belongs to the sex that cannot have babies. Boys and men are males.

◆ The opposite of male is female.

mammal *noun* (mammals)

A mammal is an animal that can feed its babies with its own milk. Dogs, cows, whales, and people are all mammals.

man *noun* (men)

A man is a fully grown male person.

◆ Some other words that end with the letters 'an' are: can pan ran van

manage *verb* (manages, managing, managed)

If you can manage, you can do something although it is difficult.

many

Many means a lot of something.

There are many stars in the sky.

map *noun* (maps)

A map is a drawing of part of the world. Maps tell you where different places are and show you things like towns, roads, rivers, and mountains.

◆ A book of maps is called an atlas.

mark *noun* (marks)

A mark is a spot or line on a surface that sometimes spoils it.

How did you get that dirty mark on your shirt?

◆ Some other words that end with the letters 'ark' are: bark dark park

marmalade *noun*

Marmalade is a jam made from oranges or lemons.

Oscar likes to eat marmalade sandwiches.

marry *verb* (marries, marrying, married)

When two people marry, they become husband and wife.

mask *noun* (masks)

A mask is a cover that you can wear over your face. People wear masks to protect their faces or to change the way they look.

a
b
c
d
e
f
g
h
i
j
k
l
m
n
o
p
q
r
s
t
u
v
w
x
y
z

mat *noun* (mats)

A mat is a piece of thick material that covers part of the floor.

◆ Some other words that end with the letters 'at' are: bat cat flat hat pat rat sat that

maths *noun*

Maths is learning about numbers, sizes, and shapes.

match *noun* (matches)

1 A match is a small, thin stick that makes a flame when it is rubbed on something rough.

2 A match is also a game played between two people or teams.

We had a football match in the garden.

match *verb* (matches, matching, matched)

If one thing matches another, it is like it in some way.

My new red shoes match my red dress.

material *noun* (materials)

1 A material is anything that can be used to make something else. Wood, stone, and plastic are materials.

2 Material is something that you can use to make things like clothes and curtains.

matter *verb* (matters, mattering, mattered)

If something matters, it is important.

It doesn't matter if we are a bit late.

mattress *noun* (mattresses)

A mattress is the thick, soft part of a bed that you sleep on.

may *verb*

1 If you may do something, you are allowed to do it.

May I have another chocolate?

2 If something may happen, it is possible it will happen.

It may rain tomorrow.

◆ Some other words that end with the letters 'ay' are: day hay lay pay play ray say stay way

94

me

Look at me.

meadow *noun* (meadows)

A meadow is a field in the country that is covered with grass.

meal *noun* (meals)

A meal is the food that you eat at one go at breakfast, lunch, dinner, tea, or supper.

◆ A picnic is a meal you eat outdoors. A feast is a special meal for a lot of people.

mean *adjective* (meaner, meanest)

1 If something you do is mean, it is not kind to someone else.

It is mean to tease your little brother.

2 Someone who is mean does not like spending money or sharing things.

Ebenezer Scrooge was a mean old man.

mean *verb* (means, meaning, meant)

1 If someone tells you what a word means, they tell you how to use it.

Do you know what the word bargain means?

2 If you mean to do something, you plan to do it.

I'm sorry — I didn't mean to hurt you.

meant SEE **mean** *verb*

I didn't know what the word exit meant.

I meant to tell you, but I forgot.

measles *noun*

Measles is an illness that makes you have red spots on your skin.

measure *verb* (measures, measuring, measured)

When you measure something, you find out how big it is.

I used a ruler to measure the length of my foot.

meat *noun*

Meat is food that comes from animals that have been killed.

◆ The word meat sounds just like meet.

Some other words that end with the letters 'eat' are: beat eat heat neat seat wheat

medicine *noun* (medicines)

Medicine is a liquid or pills that a sick person takes to help them get better.

meet *verb* (meets, meeting, met)

When people meet, they come together.

We'll meet you outside the cinema.

◆ The word meet sounds just like meat.

Some other words that end with the letters 'eet' are: feet greet sheet street sweet

a
b
c
d
e
f
g
h
i
j
k
l
m
n
o
p
q
r
s
t
u
v
w
x
y
z

melon *noun* (melons)

A melon is a large, juicy fruit with a yellow or green skin.

◆ If you mix up all the letters in the word melon, you can make the name of another fruit — lemon.

melt *verb* (melts, melting, melted)

When something melts, it turns into a liquid as it gets hotter.

My ice cream is melting in the sun.

mend *verb* (mends, mending, mended)

When you mend something that is damaged, you make it useful again.

Mum, can you help me mend my bike?

◆ Other words that mean the same as mend are repair and fix.

mess *noun*

If something is in a mess, it is untidy or dirty.

This room is in such a mess!

◆ Some other words that end with the letters 'ess' are: chess dress guess less press

message *noun* (messages)

You send a message when you want to tell someone something and you cannot speak to them yourself.

messy *adjective* (messier, messiest)

If something is messy, it is untidy or dirty.

How did this floor get so messy?

◆ The opposite of messy is tidy, neat, or clean.

met SEE **meet**

We met my uncle and aunt at the railway station.

metal *noun* (metals)

Metal is a hard material that melts when it is very hot. Gold, silver, and iron are all kinds of metal.

mice SEE **mouse**

microwave *noun* (microwaves)

A microwave is a kind of oven that heats or cooks food very quickly.

middle *noun*

The middle of something is the part that is the same distance from all its sides.

Draw a heart in the middle of the paper.

midnight *noun*

Midnight is twelve o'clock at night.

Cinderella's fairy godmother warned her to leave before midnight.

might *verb*

If something might happen, it is possible it will happen.

It might rain tomorrow.

milk *noun*

Milk is a white liquid that mothers and female mammals feed their babies with. People often drink cow's milk.

mind *noun* (minds)

Your mind is the part of you that thinks, feels, understands, and remembers.

mind *verb* (minds, minding, minded)

1 If you mind about something, you are worried or bothered by it.

Do you mind if I open the window?

2 If you mind something or somebody, you look after them for a short time.

Please mind the baby while I go next door.

3 If someone tells you to mind something, they want you to be careful.

Mind that broken glass.

mirror *noun* (mirrors)

A mirror is a piece of glass that you can see yourself in.

Mirror, mirror, on the wall, who's the fairest of them all?

◆ The word mirror comes from a Latin word that means 'to look at'.

miss *verb* (misses, missing, missed)

1 If you try to hit something and you miss, you do not hit it.

Every time I tried to hit the ball with the bat, I missed.

2 If you miss a bus or train, you do not catch it.

3 If you miss somebody, you feel sad because they are not there with you.

mistake *noun* (mistakes)

A mistake is something that you did not get right.

mix *verb* (mixes, mixing, mixed)

When you mix things, you stir or shake them until they become one thing.

Mix flour and water to make paste.

a b c d e f g h i j k l **m** n o p q r s t u v w x y z

a
b
c
d
e
f
g
h
i
j
k
l
m
n
o
p
q
r
s
t
u
v
w
x
y
z

mixture *noun* (mixtures)

A mixture is made of different things mixed together.

Paste is a mixture of flour and water.

model *noun* (models)

A model is a small copy of something.

mole *adjective* (moles)

A mole is a small, furry animal that digs tunnels under the ground.

moment *noun* (moments)

A moment is a very small amount of time.

Wait here — I'll only be a moment.

Monday *noun* (Mondays)

Monday is the second day of the week.

money *noun*

Money is the coins and paper notes that people use to buy things.

monkey *noun* (monkeys)

A monkey is an animal that lives in the trees in hot countries. It swings and climbs using its hands, feet, and long tail.

monster *noun* (monsters)

In stories, a monster is a huge, horrible creature.

◆ What do *sea* monsters eat?
Fish and ships.

month *noun* (months)

A month is part of a year. There are twelve months in a year.

◆ The twelve months of the year are January, February, March, April, May, June, July, August, September, October, November, and December.

moon *noun*

The moon moves round the Earth once every twenty-eight days. You can often see the moon shining in the sky at night.

more

More means a larger amount of something.

There is more water in a lake than a pond.

◆ The opposite of more is less.

morning *noun* (mornings)

The morning is the time from the beginning of the day until twelve o'clock noon.

mother *noun* (mothers)

A mother is a woman who has a son or daughter.

motorbike *noun* (motorbikes)

A motorbike is a kind of heavy bicycle with an engine.

motorway *noun* (motorways)

A motorway is a very wide road, made so that traffic can move fast.

mountain *noun* (mountains)

A mountain is a very high hill.

There is snow on top of the mountain.

mouse *noun* (mice)

1 A mouse is a very small animal with a long tail and a pointed nose.

The mice were dancing in the moonlight.

2 A mouse is also a small box with buttons that you press to move things around on a computer screen.

◆ The computer mouse got its name because it is small and looks like it has a long tail.

mouth *noun* (mouths)

Your mouth is the part of your face that you open for speaking and eating.

move *verb* (moves, moving, moved)

1 If you move, you go from one place to another.

Let's move under that tree. It's too hot here.

2 If you move something, you take it from one place to another.

Please move your toys off the floor.

much

Much means a lot of something.

I don't want much rice.

mud *noun*

Mud is wet earth.

We were covered in mud after playing football.

◆ Something that is covered in mud is muddy.

mug *noun* (mugs)

A mug is a large cup that does not need a saucer.

multiply *verb* (multiplies, multiplying, multiplied)

When you multiply, you find the answer to a sum like 2 × 3 =.

mum *noun* (mums)

Mum or mummy is what you call your mother.

muscle *noun* (muscles)

Muscles are the parts inside your body that help you move.

◆ The word muscle comes from a Latin word that means 'little mouse', because people thought that some muscles looked like mice.

museum *noun* (museums)

A museum is a place where a lot of interesting things are kept for people to go and see.

We went to the museum to see the dinosaur skeletons.

mushroom *noun* (mushrooms)

A mushroom is a living thing that grows in the earth and looks like a little umbrella.

music *noun*

Music is the sounds that are made by someone singing, or playing a musical instrument.

◆ A person who plays a musical instrument is called a musician.

must

If you must do something, you have to do it.

We must go now or we'll miss our bus.

my

Do you like my new watch?

myself

I have hurt myself.

a b c d e f g h i j k l **m** n o p q r s t u v w x y z

99

Nn

nail *noun* (nails)

1 A nail is the hard part that covers the end of each finger and toe.

My nails are getting very long.

2 A nail is also a small piece of metal with a sharp point. Nails are used to join pieces of wood together.

name *noun* (names)

A name is what you call someone or something.

Rumpelstiltskin is my name.

◆ Some other words that end with the letters 'ame' are: blame flame frame game same tame

narrow *adjective* (narrower, narrowest)

Something that is narrow does not measure very much from one side to the other.

There was a narrow passage between the houses.

◆ The opposite of narrow is wide.

nasty *adjective* (nastier, nastiest)

1 Something that is nasty is not at all pleasant.

What a nasty smell!

2 Someone who is nasty is not at all kind.

Don't be so nasty to your little brother.

natural *adjective*

Something that is natural has not been made by people or machines. Wool is a natural material.

nature *noun*

Nature is everything in the world that has not been made by people.

naughty *adjective* (naughtier, naughtiest)

A naughty child is one who behaves badly.

near *adjective*
(nearer, nearest)
If something is
near it is not far away.
Rapunzel sat near the window.

nearly
Nearly means very close to something.
He's nearly tall enough to reach the shelf.

◆ Little words can hide in big words. Can you see the words near, ear, and early hiding in the word nearly?

neat *adjective* (neater, neatest)
If something is neat, it is tidy and not in a mess.
Put the books into a neat pile.

◆ A word that means the same as neat is tidy.

Some other words that end with the letters 'eat' are: beat eat heat meat seat wheat

neck *noun* (necks)
Your neck is the part of your body that joins your head to your shoulders.
A giraffe has a long neck.

necklace *noun* (necklaces)
A necklace is a piece of jewellery that you wear round your neck.

need *verb* (needs, needing, needed)
1 If people need something, they cannot live and be healthy without it.
Everybody needs water to drink.
2 If you need something, you cannot manage without it.
I need another sheet of paper to finish my story.

needle *noun* (needles)
1 A needle is a very thin, pointed piece of metal. Needles used for sewing have holes in them for the thread to go through.
2 Needles can be thin rods used for knitting.
3 A needle can also be a thin leaf. Pine trees have needles.

neighbour *noun* (neighbours)
A neighbour is someone who lives near to you.

nephew *noun* (nephews)
A person's nephew is the son of their brother or sister.

nervous *adjective*
1 If you are nervous, you feel afraid and excited because of something you have to do.
I felt nervous about being in the play.
2 A person or animal that is nervous is easily frightened.
Don't go near the nest — the mother bird is very nervous.

nest *noun* (nests)
A nest is a home made by birds, mice, and some other animals for their babies.

◆ Why do birds in a nest always agree? Because they don't want to fall out.

net *noun* (nets)
A net is made of string or thread tied together with spaces in between. Nets are used in games like football and tennis. Nets are also used to catch fish and other animals.

a b c d e f g h i j k l m **n** o p q r s t u v w x y z

a
b
c
d
e
f
g
h
i
j
k
l
m
n
o
p
q
r
s
t
u
v
w
x
y
z

never

Never means not at any time.

Grace is excited because she has never been on a plane.

new *adjective* (newer, newest)

1 Something that is new has just been bought or made.

I got a new bike for my birthday.

2 New can mean different.

I'm starting at a new school tomorrow.

◆ The opposite of new is old.

news *noun*

News is information about what has just happened.

Have you heard the news? We won the match!

newspaper *noun* (newspapers)

A newspaper is a number of large sheets of paper folded together, with the news printed on them. Most newspapers come out every day.

newt *noun* (newts)

A newt is a small animal that looks like a lizard and lives near water.

next

1 Next means the one coming after this one.

Please turn over to the next page.

2 Next means the one nearest to you.

Look who's sitting at the next table.

nice *adjective* (nicer, nicest)

If somebody or something is nice, you like them.

Our new teacher is very nice.

◆ Some other words that end with the letters 'ice' are: dice ice mice price rice

niece *noun* (nieces)

A person's niece is the daughter of their brother or sister.

night *noun* (nights)

Night is the time when it is dark, after the sun goes down.

◆ The word night sounds just like knight.

Some other words that end with the letters 'ight' are: bright fight fright light right tight

nightdress *noun* (nightdresses)

A nightdress is a kind of long, loose dress that girls and women wear in bed.

nightmare *noun* (nightmares)

A nightmare is a frightening dream.

nine *noun* (nines)

Nine is the number 9.

no

'Can I have another chocolate?' 'No'.
There are no fish in the pond.

nod *verb* (nods, nodding, nodded)

When you nod, you move your head down and then up again quickly, to show that you agree.

noise *noun* (noises)

A noise is a loud sound that someone or something makes.

The big truck made a lot of noise as it went by.

noisy *adjective* (noisier, noisiest)

A lot of loud sound is noisy.

◆ A word that means the same as noisy is loud.

nonsense *noun*

Nonsense is something that someone says that is silly or does not mean anything.

What a lot of nonsense you talk!

noon *noun*

Noon is twelve o'clock in the middle of the day.

◆ Noon is a word that is spelled the same forwards or backwards. A word like this is called a palindrome.

north *noun*

North is a direction. If you face towards the place where the sun comes up in the morning, north is on your left.

nose *noun* (noses)

Your nose is the part of your face that you use for breathing and smelling.

Whenever Pinocchio told a lie, his nose grew longer.

not

I am not hungry.

◆ The word not sounds just like knot.

note *noun* (notes)

1 A note is a short letter.

Mum left a note on the door saying she would be back soon.

2 A note is also one sound in music.

notice *verb* (notices, noticing, noticed)

If you notice something, you see it and think about it.

Did you notice those funny socks he was wearing?

notice *noun* (notices)

A notice is a piece of paper or board that tells people something.

The notice said 'No dogs allowed'.

now

Now means at this time.

What time is it now?

number *noun* (numbers)

Numbers tell you how many people or things there are.

Numbers can be written as words (one, two, three), or as signs (1, 2, 3).

nurse *noun* (nurses)

A nurse is someone whose job is to take care of people who are ill or hurt.

nut *noun* (nuts)

A nut is a kind of dry fruit that you can eat after you have taken off its hard shell.

Monkeys love to eat nuts.

a b c d e f g h i j k l m **n** o p q r s t u v w x y z

Oo

oar *noun* (oars)

An oar is a long pole with a flat part at one end. You use oars to row a boat.

oat *noun* (oats)

Oats are the seeds of a cereal plant. They are used as food for people and animals.

obey *verb* (obeys, obeying, obeyed)

When you obey, you do what someone tells you.

That dog always obeys his owner.

ocean *noun* (oceans)

An ocean is a very big sea.

The Pacific Ocean is the biggest ocean in the world.

◆ If you mix up all the letters in the word ocean, you can make the word canoe.

octopus *noun* (octopuses)

An octopus is a sea animal with eight long arms and a soft body.

◆ The word octopus comes from a Greek word that means 'eight feet'.

odd *adjective* (odder, oddest)

1 If something is odd, it seems strange.

That's odd! There was a snowman here a minute ago and now it's gone.

2 An odd number cannot be divided by two without having something left over. 7, 13, and 27 are odd numbers.

3 Odd things do not belong in a pair.

Uncle David is wearing odd socks.

of

This is a picture of my pet mouse.

off

The big Billy Goat Gruff pushed the troll off the bridge.

offer *verb* (offers, offering, offered)

1 If you offer something, you ask someone if they would like it.

The witch offered Snow White an apple.

2 If you offer to do something, you do not wait to be asked.

I offered to help wash the dishes.

often

If something happens often, it happens a lot.

We often go to the park on Saturdays.

oil *noun*

Oil is a thick, slippery liquid. It can be burned to keep people warm, or put on machines to help them move easily. Some kinds of oil are used in cooking.

old *adjective* (older, oldest)

1 Someone who is old was born a long time ago.

My grandfather is very old.

2 Something that is old was made a long time ago.

This Greek vase is very old.

3 You say something is old if you have had it a long time.

My old shoes are not as nice as my new ones.

◆ The opposite of the first meaning of old is young. The opposite of the other meanings of old is new.

Some other words that end with the letters 'old' are: bold cold fold gold hold sold told

105

on

Peter put his shoes on.

once

Once upon a time, there lived a girl called Thumbelina.

one *noun*

One is the number 1.

only

There are only two chocolates left.

open *adjective*

When something is open, people or things can go into it or through it.

Can you hold the door open, please?

open *verb* (opens, opening, opened)

If you open something, you make it no longer shut or closed.

The prince opened the door with a golden key.

◆ The opposite of open is close or shut.

opposite *noun* (opposites)

The opposite of something is the thing that is as different from it as possible.

Tall is the opposite of short.

opposite

If something is opposite something else, it is on the other side.

When you play chess, you sit opposite the other player.

106

or

Do you want cream or custard?

orange *noun* (oranges)

An orange is a round and sweet fruit with a thick peel.

orange *adjective*

Orange is the colour of carrots and oranges.

orchestra *noun* (orchestras)

An orchestra is a large group of people playing musical instruments together.

order *noun*

Order is the way something is arranged.

The animals on this page are arranged in order of their size.

order *verb* (orders, ordering, ordered)

1 If someone orders you to do something, they say you have to do it.

The general ordered his men to attack.

2 If you order something in a restaurant, you say that is what you want.

Mum ordered a chicken sandwich.

ordinary *adjective*

Ordinary things are not special in any way.

To begin with, it was just an ordinary day.

other

Other means not this one.

Where is my other shoe?

our

This is our house.

out

Salik gently took the rabbit out of the hutch.

outside

Outside means not inside a building.

Mum, please can I play outside?

oven *noun* (ovens)

An oven is the space inside a cooker where food can be baked.

Put the cake in the oven and bake it for half an hour.

over

Over means above or on top of.

The cow jumped over the moon.

◆ The opposite of over is under.

owe *verb* (owes, owing, owed)

If you owe money to someone, you have not yet paid them.

I owe you the three pounds I borrowed last week.

owl *noun* (owls)

An owl is a bird with a large, round head and large eyes. Owls hunt small animals at night.

The owl slowly turned its head almost all the way round.

own *verb* (owns, owning, owned)

1 If you own something, it is yours.

Does anyone here own a red watch?

2 If you own up, you say that you were the one who did something.

Who will own up to breaking the window?

Pp

paddle *verb* (paddles, paddling, paddled)

When you paddle, you walk about in water that is not very deep.

page *noun* (pages)

A page is one side of a piece of paper in a book.

pain *noun* (pains)

Pain is the feeling you have when part of your body hurts.

I've got a pain in my ear.

◆ Some other words that end with the letters 'ain' are: brain chain drain grain main rain train

paint *noun* (paints)

Paint is a liquid that you put on the surface of something to colour it.

paint *verb* (paints, painting, painted)

1 If you paint a picture, you make a coloured picture with paints.

2 If someone paints something like a door, they put paint on to it.

painting *noun* (paintings)

A painting is a picture that someone has painted.

pair *noun* (pairs)

1 A pair is two people, two animals, or two things that belong together.

I bought Dad a pair of orange socks for his birthday.

2 Things like trousers and scissors are also called a pair, because they have two parts joined together.

Have you got a pair of scissors?

◆ The word pair sounds just like pear.

Some other words that end with the letters 'air' are: air chair fair hair stair

palace *noun* (palaces)

A palace is a very large, grand house where people like kings and queens live.

The Snow Queen lived in a palace of ice.

pale *adjective* (paler, palest)

Something that is pale in colour is almost white.

You look very pale. Do you feel all right?

palm *noun* (palms)

1 Your palm is the inside of your hand between your fingers and your wrist.

2 A palm is a tree that grows in hot countries. It has large leaves and no branches.

panda *noun* (pandas)

A panda is a large animal with black and white fur that looks like a bear.

panic *noun*

Panic is sudden fear that you cannot control.

People saw the smoke and got into a panic.

pant *verb* (pants, panting, panted)

When you pant, you take short, quick breaths.

He could hear the dog panting up the hill behind him.

pantomime *noun* (pantomimes)

A pantomime is a kind of play. It tells a fairy story, and has songs and jokes in it.

paper *noun* (papers)

1 Paper is a very thin material that is used for things like making books, and for writing on and for wrapping things up.

2 Paper is also short for newspaper.

Mum was reading the paper.

a
b
c
d
e
f
g
h
i
j
k
l
m
n
o
p
q
r
s
t
u
v
w
x
y
z

109

a
b
c
d
e
f
g
h
i
j
k
l
m
n
o
p
q
r
s
t
u
v
w
x
y
z

parachute

noun (parachutes)

A parachute is used to help people float slowly down to the ground after jumping out of an aeroplane. It is made of a large piece of material that looks like a huge umbrella.

parcel *noun* (parcels)

A parcel is something that is wrapped up so that it can be posted or given to someone as a present.

parent *noun* (parents)

Your parents are your mother and father.

park *noun* (parks)

A park is a large piece of land with grass and trees where anyone can walk or play.

park *verb* (parks, parking, parked)

When people park a car, they leave it somewhere for a short time.

◆ Some other words that end with the letters 'ark' are: bark dark mark

parrot *noun* (parrots)

A parrot is a bird with brightly coloured feathers and a large, curved beak.

Does your parrot talk?

part *noun* (parts)

A part is anything that belongs to something bigger.

A roof is part of a house.

party *noun* (parties)

A party is when a group of people come together to enjoy themselves.

pass *verb* (passes, passing, passed)

1 If you pass something, you go by it.

I pass your school every day.

2 If you pass something to someone, you give it to them with your hand.

Pass the butter, please.

3 If you pass a test, you do well.

My sister has passed her driving test.

passenger *noun* (passengers)

A passenger is anyone travelling in a car, bus, train, ship, or aeroplane.

past *noun*

The past is the time before now.

In the past, soldiers wore armour to protect them.

pasta *noun*

Pasta is food made from flour, eggs, and water, that is made into shapes. You cook pasta in boiling water and eat it with sauce.

paste *noun*

Paste is a thick, wet mixture that you can use to stick paper to things.

pastry *noun*

Pastry is a mixture of flour, fat, and water which has been rolled and baked.

path *noun* (paths)

A path is a narrow way that you can go along.

Follow the path through the forest.

patient *adjective*

If you are patient, you can wait for a long time, or do something difficult, without getting angry.

patient *noun* (patients)

A patient is someone who is ill and is being cared for by a doctor.

pattern *noun* (patterns)

A pattern is the way something is arranged, like lines and shapes on material, or sounds in music.

paw *noun* (paws)

A paw is an animal's foot.

The dog has hurt its paw.

pay *verb* (pays, paying, paid)

To pay means to give money for work or for things you have bought.

◆ Some other words that end with the letters 'ay' are: day hay lay may play ray say stay way

PE *noun*

PE is exercises that you do to keep your body healthy.

pea *noun* (peas)

Peas are small, round, green vegetables that grow in pods.

pear *noun* (pears)

A pear is a green or yellow fruit that is bigger at the bottom than the top.

◆ The word pear sounds just like pair.

pebble *noun* (pebbles)

A pebble is a small, smooth stone you find on the beach.

111

a
b
c
d
e
f
g
h
i
j
k
l
m
n
o
p
q
r
s
t
u
v
w
x
y
z

pedal *noun* (pedals)

A pedal is a part that you press with your foot to make something work. A bicycle has two pedals.

peel *noun*

Peel is the skin on some fruit and vegetables.

pen *noun* (pens)

A pen is something you use to write with in ink.

pencil *noun* (pencils)

A pencil is a long, thin stick with black or a colour right through the middle. You use a pencil for writing or drawing.

penguin *noun* (penguins)

A penguin is a black and white bird that usually lives in very cold places. Penguins cannot fly but are good swimmers.

people *noun*

People are men, women, and children.

pepper *noun*

Pepper is a powder that you add to food to give it a hot taste.

perch *verb* (perches, perching, perched)

When you perch on something, you sit on the edge of it, like a bird on a branch.

period *noun* (periods)

A period is a length of time.
There will be short periods of rain all day.

person *noun* (people)

A person is a man, woman, or child.

pest *noun* (pests)

A pest is any person, animal, or plant that is a lot of trouble.
Flies are a real pest when you're having a picnic.

pet *noun* (pets)

A pet is a tame animal that you keep in your home. Cats and dogs are often kept as pets.

petal *noun* (petals)

A petal is a coloured part of a flower.

◆ The word petal comes from a Greek word that means 'a leaf'.

phone *noun* (phones)

Phone is short for telephone.

photo *noun* (photos)

A photo is a picture taken with a camera. Photo is short for photograph.

piano *noun* (pianos)

A piano is a large musical instrument. It has black and white keys that you press down with your fingers.

pick *verb* (picks, picking, picked)

1 If you pick somebody or something, you decide which one you want.

Salik picked three of his friends to be in his team.

2 If you pick a thing up, you lift it.

Can you pick up that basket, please?

3 If you pick flowers, fruit, or vegetables, you take them from where they are growing.

◆ Some other words that end with the letters 'ick' are: brick chick click flick kick lick quick sick stick thick trick

picnic *noun* (picnics)

A picnic is a meal you eat outdoors.

picture *noun* (pictures)

A picture is a painting, drawing, or photograph.

pie *noun* (pies)

A pie is meat or fruit covered with pastry and baked in an oven.

piece *noun* (pieces)

A piece of something is part of it.

Would you like a piece of apple pie?

pier *noun* (piers)

A pier is a long, thin platform that goes out over the sea.

113

a
b
c
d
e
f
g
h
i
j
k
l
m
n
o
p
q
r
s
t
u
v
w
x
y
z

pig *noun* (pigs)

A pig is an animal that is kept on a farm for its meat. Pigs have short, flat noses, called snouts, and curly tails.

◆ A baby pig is called a piglet.

pigeon *noun* (pigeons)

A pigeon is a bird with a fat body and small head. Pigeons are often seen in cities.

pile *noun* (piles)

A pile is a number of things put on top of one another.

Jason was carrying a pile of books.

pill *noun* (pills)

A pill is a small, round piece of medicine that can be swallowed whole.

◆ Some other words that end with the letters 'ill' are: bill fill hill ill kill still till will

pillow *noun* (pillows)

A pillow is something soft that you rest your head on in bed.

◆ Little words can hide in big words. Can you see the words pill, ill, and low hiding in the word pillow?

pilot *noun* (pilots)

A pilot is a person who flies an aeroplane.

pin *noun* (pins)

A pin is a short, thin piece of metal with a sharp point at one end. You use pins to hold pieces of paper or cloth together.

◆ Some other words that end with the letters 'in' are: bin chin spin thin tin twin win

pink *adjective*

Pink is a colour made by mixing red and white.

pipe

noun (pipes)

A pipe is a long, thin tube that carries gas or water.

pirate *noun* (pirates)

A pirate is a sailor who attacks and robs other ships at sea.

pizza *noun* (pizzas)

A pizza is a large, flat pie covered with cheese, tomatoes, and other foods. You bake pizza quickly in a very hot oven.

place *noun* (places)

A place is a particular part of a space or building.

Here's a good place for a picnic.

◆ Some other words that end with the letters 'ace' are: face lace race space

plain *adjective* (plainer, plainest)

1 Something that is plain does not have a pattern on it.

Hannah was wearing a plain, blue T-shirt.

2 If something is plain, it is easy to see or understand.

It is plain that you haven't been listening.

◆ The word plain sounds just like plane.

plan *verb* (plans, planning, planned)

When you plan something, you decide what is going to be done.

Alex and Sarah are planning their magic show.

plane *noun* (planes)

Plane is short for aeroplane.

◆ The word plane sounds just like plain.

planet *noun* (planets)

A planet is any of the worlds in space that move around a star.

The Earth, Mars, and Saturn are some of the planets that go around the Sun.

◆ Little words can hide in big words. Can you see the words plan, plane, lane, an, and net hiding in the word planet?

plant *noun* (plants)

A plant is anything that grows out of the ground. Trees, bushes, and flowers are all plants.

plaster *noun* (plasters)

1 A plaster is a sticky strip of material for covering cuts.

2 Plaster is a soft mixture that goes hard when it dries. Plaster is used to cover the walls inside buildings.

plastic *noun*

Plastic is a light, strong material that is made in factories. It is used to make bottles, bowls, buckets, toys, and many other things.

plate *noun* (plates)

A plate is a flat dish that you put food on.

◆ Some other words that end with the letters 'ate' are: date gate hate late

platform *noun* (platforms)

1 A platform is part of a room that is higher than the rest.

The children went up to the platform to get their prizes.

2 A platform is also the place in a station where people wait for a train.

play *verb* (plays, playing, played)

1 When you play, you do something for fun.

Can we play in the garden?

2 When you play a sport or game, you spend time trying to win it.

3 If you play a musical instrument, you make music with it.

◆ Some other words that end with the letters 'ay' are: day hay lay may pay ray say stay way

playground *noun* (playgrounds)

A playground is a place outside where children can play. Playgrounds often have swings, slides, and things to climb on.

◆ Little words can hide in big words. Can you see the words play, lay, ground, and round hiding in the word playground?

a b c d e f g h i j k l m n o **p** q r s t u v w x y z

a
b
c
d
e
f
g
h
i
j
k
l
m
n
o
p
q
r
s
t
u
v
w
x
y
z

pleasant *adjective*
(pleasanter, pleasantest)
1 Pleasant people are nice to be with.
2 If something is pleasant, you enjoy it.

please *verb* (pleases, pleasing, pleased)
1 If somebody or something pleases you, they make you feel happy.
I was pleased to see my friend.
2 You say please to ask for something politely.
Please may I have some juice?

plenty *noun*
If there is plenty of something, there is more than you need.
Help yourself to more popcorn. There's plenty for everyone.

plum *noun* (plums)
A plum is a juicy fruit with a stone in the middle. Plums have dark red or purple skin.

pocket *noun* (pockets)
A pocket is a small bag that is sewn into your clothes, for keeping things in.

poem *noun* (poems)
A poem is a piece of writing with a special rhythm. Poems usually have short lines and the words at the end of the lines often rhyme.
◆ A person who writes poems is called a poet.

point
noun (points)
1 A point is the sharp end of things like pins and pencils.
2 A point is also part of the score in a game.
That's one point to me!

point *verb* (points, pointing, pointed)
When you point, you show where something is by holding out your finger towards it.

pointed *adjective*
Something pointed has a sharp point at the end.

poisonous *adjective*
Poisonous things would make you ill or kill you if you swallowed them.
Snow White ate the poisonous apple.

a b c d e f g h i j k l m n o **p** q r s t u v w x y z

pond *noun* (ponds)

A pond is a small lake.

pony *noun* (ponies)

A pony is a small horse.

pool *noun* (pools)

A pool is a small area of water.

poor *adjective* (poorer, poorest)

1 Someone who is poor does not have much money.

2 Poor can also mean not very good.

It is difficult to read in this poor light.

◆ The opposite of the first meaning of poor is rich.

porridge *noun*

Porridge is a hot breakfast food, made from oats boiled in water or milk.

possible *adjective*

If something is possible, it can happen or be done.

Is it possible to get there by bus?

polar bear *noun* (polar bears)

A polar bear is a large white bear that lives near the North Pole.

police *noun*

The police are the people whose job is to see that no one breaks the law.

◆ A person who is one of the police is called a police officer.

polite *adjective* (politer, politest)

Someone who is polite is well behaved.

It is polite to say 'please' when you ask for something.

◆ The opposite of polite is rude.

a
b
c
d
e
f
g
h
i
j
k
l
m
n
o
p
q
r
s
t
u
v
w
x
y
z

post *noun* (posts)

1 A post is an upright pole fixed in the ground.

2 The post is the letters or parcels that are delivered to your home.

Did we get any post today?

post *verb* (posts, posting, posted)

If you post something like a letter, you send it in the post.

I posted a card to Granny yesterday.

poster *noun* (posters)

A poster is a large picture or notice for everyone to read.

potato *noun* (potatoes)

A potato is a vegetable that grows in the ground. Crisps and chips are made from potatoes.

pour *verb* (pours, pouring, poured)

When you pour a liquid, you make it run out of something like a bottle or jug.

Mum poured some juice into the glasses.

powder *noun* (powders)

Powder is something that is made up of very tiny pieces, like dust or flour.

power *noun*

The power of something is the strength that it has.

The animals were frightened by the power of the storm.

practise *verb* (practises, practising, practised)

When you practise something, you keep doing it so that you get better at it.

I practise the piano every day.

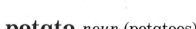

present

noun (presents)

1 A present is something special you give to someone.

2 The present is the time right now.

Dad's not at home at present.

present *adjective*

Someone who is present is in a particular place.

The mayor was present at the opening of the new school.

president *noun* (presidents)

A president is someone who is chosen to lead a country.

press *verb* (presses, pressing, pressed)

When you press something, you push hard on it.

Tom pressed the button at the crossing.

◆ Some other words that end with the letters 'ess' are: chess dress guess less mess

prey *noun*

Prey is any animal hunted and eaten by another animal.

The eagle dived on to its prey.

price *noun* (prices)

The price of something is how much money you have to pay to buy it.

◆ Some other words that end with the letters 'ice' are: dice ice mice nice rice

prick *verb* (pricks, pricking, pricked)

If you prick something, you make a tiny hole with a sharp point.

The princess pricked her finger on the needle.

pretend *verb* (pretends, pretending, pretended)

When you pretend, you act as though something is true when it is not really.

Emma is pretending to be a ghost.

pretty *adjective* (prettier, prettiest)

Pretty means nice to look at.

What pretty flowers!

prince *noun* (princes)

A prince is the son of a king or queen.

princess *noun* (princesses)

1 A princess is the daughter of a king or queen.
2 The wife of a prince is also called a princess.

prison *noun* (prisons)

A prison is a place where people are kept as a punishment for breaking the law.

a b c d e f g h i j k l m n o **p** q r s t u v w x y z

a
b
c
d
e
f
g
h
i
j
k
l
m
n
o
p
q
r
s
t
u
v
w
x
y
z

prize *noun* (prizes)

A prize is something you get for winning or for doing something well.

problem *noun* (problems)

A problem is something that is hard to understand or to deal with.

Hold on, we've got a problem. The torch doesn't work.

programme *noun* (programmes)

1 A programme is a show on radio or television.

2 A programme is also a list that tells an audience what is going to happen.

project *noun* (projects)

When you do a project, you find out as much as you can about something and then write about it.

We're doing a project on dinosaurs.

promise *verb* (promises, promising, promised)

When you promise, you say you will really do or not do something.

I promise I won't do it again.

proper *adjective*

Proper means right.

I need the proper tool for this job.

protect *verb* (protects, protecting, protected)

If someone or something protects you, they keep you safe from harm.

You should wear a helmet to protect your head when you ride your bike.

proud *adjective* (prouder, proudest)

If you feel proud, you are very pleased because you or someone close to you has done well.

I was proud of my brother when he won the race.

◆ When you are proud, you feel a sense of pride.

pudding *noun* (puddings)

A pudding is something sweet like apple pie or trifle. You eat it at the end of a meal.

My favourite pudding is jelly and ice cream.

puddle *noun* (puddles)

A puddle is a small pool of water.

pull *verb* (pulls, pulling, pulled)

When you pull something, you get hold of it and make it come towards you.

◆ The opposite of pull is push.

puncture *noun* (punctures)

A puncture is a small hole in a tyre.

punishment *noun* (punishments)

A punishment is something that is done to someone who has done wrong.

pupil *noun* (pupils)

1 A pupil is someone who is being taught something.

2 Your pupils are the black spots in the middle of your eyes.

puppet *noun* (puppet)

A puppet is a kind of doll that can be made to move. Some puppets are put on like gloves, and you work them with your fingers. Others are moved with strings from above.

puppy *noun* (puppies)

A puppy is a young dog.

pure *adjective* (purer, purest)

Something that is pure does not have anything else mixed with it.

Pure orange juice has no sugar or water added to it.

purple *adjective*

Purple is a colour made by mixing blue and red.

Polly is picking purple plums.

purse *noun* (purses)

A purse is a small bag for carrying money.

push *verb* (pushes, pushing, pushed)

When you push something, you use your hands to move it away from you.

◆ The opposite of push is pull.

put *verb* (puts, putting, put)

When you put something somewhere, you move it there or leave it there.

Where did you put your coat?

puzzle *noun* (puzzles)

A puzzle is a game or a question that is hard to work out.

Do you like doing crossword puzzles?

pyjamas *noun*

Pyjamas are a pair of trousers and a loose jacket that you wear in bed.

◆ The word pyjamas comes from two Persian words that means 'leg clothes'.

a b c d e f g h i j k l m n o **p** q r s t u v w x y z

Qq

quack *verb* (quacks, quacking, quacked)

When a duck quacks, it makes a noise through its beak.

◆ Some other words that end with the letters 'ack' are: back black crack pack sack

quarrel *verb* (quarrels, quarrelling, quarrelled)

When people quarrel, they talk angrily and sometimes fight.

Mina and Katie sometimes quarrel about whose turn it is to play on the computer.

◆ Another word that means the same as quarrel is argue.

quarry *noun* (quarries)

A quarry is a place where people cut stone for buildings.

queen *noun* (queens)

1 A queen is a woman who was born to rule a country.

2 A king's wife is also called a queen.

question *noun* (questions)

A question is something you ask when you want to find something out.

quetzal *noun* (quetzals)

A quetzal is a bird that has very bright green and red feathers and very long tail feathers.

queue *noun* (queues)

A queue is a line of people waiting for something.

There was a long queue outside the cinema.

quick *adjective* (quicker, quickest)

1 Something quick is done in a short time.

Let me have a quick look at your comic.

2 To be quick means to move fast.

If we're quick, we'll be able to catch the bus.

◆ If something is quick, it happens quickly.

Another word that means the same as quick is fast.

The opposite of quick is slow.

Some other words that end with the letters 'ick' are: brick chick click flick kick lick pick sick stick thick trick

quiet *adjective* (quieter, quietest)

If someone or something is quiet, they make very little noise, or no noise at all.

Grace kept very quiet at the end of the sofa.

◆ The opposite of quiet is loud or noisy.

quite

1 If something is quite good, it is good but not special.

2 Not quite means nearly.

The potatoes are not quite cooked yet.

quiz *noun* (quizzes)

A quiz is a kind of game or test. People try to answer questions to show how much they know.

Rr

rabbit *noun* (rabbits)

A rabbit is a small, furry animal with long ears. Rabbits live in holes in the ground.

race *noun* (races)

A race is a way of finding out who is the fastest.

The tortoise and the hare decided to have a race.

◆ Some other words that end with the letters 'ace' are: face lace place space

radiator *noun* (radiators)

A radiator is made of metal, and is filled with hot water to heat a room.

radio *noun* (radios)

A radio is a machine that receives sounds sent through the air. You can listen to music, programmes, or messages on a radio.

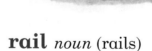

rail *noun* (rails)

1 A rail is a bar joined to posts to make something like a fence.

You can hold on to the rail by the side of the steps.

2 A rail is also a long metal bar that is part of a railway line.

railway *noun* (railways)

A railway is a set of rails for trains to run on.

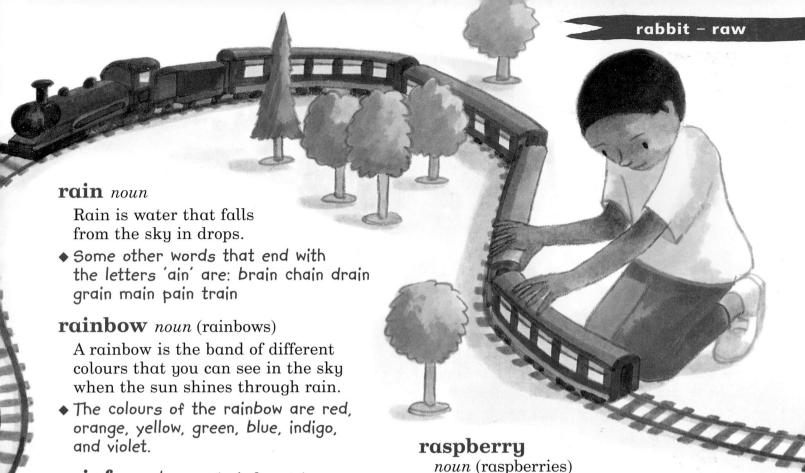

rain *noun*

Rain is water that falls from the sky in drops.

◆ Some other words that end with the letters 'ain' are: brain chain drain grain main pain train

rainbow *noun* (rainbows)

A rainbow is the band of different colours that you can see in the sky when the sun shines through rain.

◆ The colours of the rainbow are red, orange, yellow, green, blue, indigo, and violet.

rainforest *noun* (rainforests)

A rainforest is a thick forest in a warm part of the world where a lot of rain falls.

◆ Little words can hide in big words. Can you *see* the words rain, in, for, forest, or, and rest hiding in the word rainforest?

ran SEE run

Hickory, dickory, dock, the mouse ran up the clock.

◆ Some other words that end with the letters 'an' are: can gran man pan van

rang SEE ring *verb*

Melissa rang the doorbell.

rare *adjective* (rarer, rarest)

Something that is rare is not often found, or does not often happen.

Owl and Rabbit decided the flowers must be very rare.

raspberry
noun (raspberries)

A raspberry is a small, soft, red fruit.

rat *noun* (rats)

A rat looks like a mouse, but is larger.

◆ Some other words that end with the letters 'at' are: bat cat flat hat mat pat sat that

rather

1 Rather means a little bit.

Everyone said the duckling was rather ugly.

2 You say you would rather do something if you would like to do it more than something else.

I would rather watch the other channel.

raw *adjective*

Raw food is not cooked.

You can eat raw carrots in a salad.

◆ The word raw sounds just like roar.

125

a b c d e f g h i j k l m n o p q **r** s t u v w x y z

reach *verb* (reaches, reaching, reached)

1 To reach means to stretch out your hand to touch something.

If I stand on tiptoe I can just reach the top shelf.

2 To reach also means to arrive at a place.

Dorothy and her friends reached the Emerald City.

read *verb* (reads, reading, read)

When you read, you can understand words that are written down.

ready *adjective*

If you are ready, you can do something right away.

Are you ready to go?

real *adjective*

1 Something that is real is not a copy.

Are those flowers real or made of paper?

2 Real also means true and not made up.

Was Robin Hood a real person?

really

Really means you are telling the truth, or you want to hear the truth.

Do you really have a pet snake?

reason *noun* (reasons)

A reason explains why something happens or why you want to do something.

The reason I am late is that I missed the bus.

receive *verb* (receives, receiving, received)

To receive means to get something that has been given or sent to you.

I received your letter yesterday.

record *noun* (records)

1 A record is a flat, round piece of plastic. It makes music or other sounds when it turns round on a record player.

2 A record is also the best that has been done so far.

I got dressed in record time today.

record *verb* (records, recording, recorded)

When you record something, you write it down or put it on tape or a CD.

Did you record that programme?

recorder *noun* (recorders)

A recorder is a musical instrument. You play it by blowing into one end and covering holes with your fingers.

red *adjective*

Red is the colour of tomatoes and strawberries.

reflection *noun* (reflections)

A reflection is what you see in a mirror, or in anything smooth and shiny.

refrigerator *noun* (refrigerators)

A refrigerator is a metal cupboard that uses electricity to keep food cold and fresh.

◆ A refrigerator is often called a fridge for short.

refuse *verb* (refuses, refusing, refused)

If you refuse, you say you will not do something you have been asked to do.

Jamie refused to come down from the tree.

remember *verb* (remembers, remembering, remembered)

To remember means to bring something back into your mind when you want to.

I can remember the names of all the planets.

◆ The opposite of remember is forget.

remind *verb* (reminds, reminding, reminded)

If you remind somebody of something, you help them to remember it.

remove *verb* (removes, removing, removed)

If you remove something, you take it away.

A rubber will remove pencil marks.

repair *verb* (repairs, repairing, repaired)

When someone repairs something, they make it work properly again.

A man came to repair the washing machine.

◆ Other words that mean the same as repair are mend and fix.

reply *verb* (replies, replying, replied)

When you reply, you give an answer.

Have you replied to Amy's party invitation?

reptile *noun* (reptiles)

Reptiles are animals with cold blood. They have scaly skins, and short legs or no legs at all. Reptiles lay eggs.

◆ There are many different types of reptile. Here are some of them: alligator, crocodile, lizard, snake, tortoise, turtle.

The word reptile comes from a Latin word that means 'creeping'.

rescue *verb* (rescues, rescuing, rescued)

If you rescue somebody, you save them from danger.

Firefighters rescued everyone from the burning house.

rest *verb* (rests, resting, rested)

When you rest, you lie down or sit quietly.

rest *noun*

The rest is the part that is left.

I've done most of my homework. I'll do the rest tomorrow.

result *noun* (results)

A result is anything that happens because of other things.

We were late, and as a result we missed the bus.

return *verb* (returns, returning, returned)

1 If you return, you go back to where you were before.

2 If you return something, you give it back.

reward *noun* (rewards)

A reward is given to you for something good that you have done.

John was able to choose a video as a reward for clearing up his room.

rhinoceros *noun* (rhinoceroses)

A rhinoceros is a very large, heavy animal with thick skin. Rhinoceroses have one or two horns on their noses.

◆ A rhinoceros is called a rhino for short.

The word rhinoceros comes from two Greek words that mean 'nose' and 'horn'.

rhyme *verb* (rhymes, rhyming, rhymed)

Words that rhyme have the same sound at the end, like bat and cat.

rhythm *noun* (rhythms)

Rhythm is a repeated pattern of sounds in music or poetry.

ribbon *noun* (ribbons)

A ribbon is a thin strip of coloured material used to tie round hair or gifts.

rice *noun*

Rice is a white food that comes from the seeds of a kind of grass. Rice is the main food for many people in the world.

◆ Some other words that end with the letters 'ice' are: dice ice mice nice price

rich *adjective* (richer, richest)

People who are rich have a lot of money.

◆ The opposite of rich is poor.

ridden SEE **ride**

Have you ridden your new bike yet?

riddle *noun* (riddles)

A riddle is a kind of question that has a funny or clever answer.

Milo had to answer a riddle to escape from the dragon.

ride *verb* (rides, riding, rode, ridden)

1 When you ride a bicycle or a horse, you sit on it as it goes along.

2 When you ride in something like a car or train, you travel in it.

◆ Some other words that end with the letters 'ide' are: bride hide pride side tide wide

right *adjective*

If something is right, there are no mistakes in it or it is just as it should be.

◆ The opposite of right is wrong.

right *noun*

Right is the side that is opposite the left.

◆ The word right sounds just like write.

Some other words that end with the letters 'ight' are: bright fight fright light night tight

ring *noun* (rings)

1 A ring is a circle.

The children sat in a ring around the storyteller.

2 A ring can be a circle of thin metal that you wear on your finger.

3 A ring is also the sound a bell makes.

ring *verb* (rings, ringing, rang, rung)

When something rings, it makes the sound of a bell.

◆ Some other words that end with the letters 'ing' are: bring king sing sting string swing thing wing

rise *verb* (rises, rising, rose, risen)

When something rises, it goes upwards. When the sun rises it appears above the horizon.

river *noun* (rivers)

A river is a lot of water that moves naturally and flows across the land to the sea or to a lake.

◆ Why is a river lazy?
Because it never gets out of its bed.

road *noun* (roads)

A road is a way between places, made for cars and buses, bicycles, and trucks.

roar *verb* (roars, roaring, roared)

To roar is to make a loud, deep sound, like a lion makes.

◆ The word roar sounds just like raw.

robin *noun* (robins)

A robin is a small brown bird with a red breast.

a b c d e f g h i j k l m n o p q **r** s t u v w x y z

robot *noun* (robots)

A robot is a machine that can make some of the movements that a person can. In factories, robots can do some jobs that people find boring.

rock *noun* (rocks)

Rock is the hard, stony part of the earth. A rock is a piece of this.

rock *verb* (rocks, rocking, rocked)

If something rocks, it moves gently from side to side.

I hope the boat doesn't rock too much.

rocket *noun* (rockets)

1 A rocket is part of a spacecraft. Hot gases rush from the end of the rocket and move the spacecraft upwards.

2 A rocket is also a kind of firework. When it is lit, it shoots high in the air.

rode SEE **ride**

The queen rode a beautiful white horse.

roll *noun* (rolls)

1 A roll of something like tape is a very long piece of it wrapped round and round lots of times.

We need a new roll of paper towels.

2 A roll is also a small, round piece of bread made for one person.

roof *noun* (roofs)

A roof is the part that covers the top of a building or vehicle.

room *noun* (rooms)

A room is one of the spaces with walls round it in a building. A room has a floor, ceiling, and its own door.

root *noun* (roots)

A root is the part of a plant that grows under the ground.

rope *noun* (ropes)

Rope is a lot of strong threads twisted together.

rose *noun* (roses)

A rose is a flower with thorns on its stem. Roses often smell very nice.

rose SEE **rise**

Black smoke rose from the bonfire.

rough *adjective* (rougher, roughest)

1 Something that is rough is not smooth.

2 If people are rough, they are not gentle.

round *adjective* (rounder, roundest)

Round means shaped like a circle or a ball.

round

Round means on all sides of something.

There is a wall round the garden.

row *noun* (rows)

A row is a line of people or things.

row *verb* (rows, rowing, rowed)

When you row, you use oars to make a boat move through water.

royal *adjective*

Royal means to do with a king or a queen.

rub *verb* (rubs, rubbing, rubbed)

If you rub something, you press your hand on it and move it backwards and forwards.

Aladdin rubbed the lamp and a genie appeared.

rubber *noun* (rubbers)

1 Rubber is strong material that stretches, bends, and bounces. Rubber is used to make things like tyres and wellington boots.

2 A rubber is a small piece of soft rubber that you use to rub out pencil marks.

rubbish *noun*

Rubbish is things that are not wanted, like empty cans and waste paper.

ruby *noun* (rubies)

A ruby is a red jewel.

rude *adjective* (ruder, rudest)

Someone who is rude behaves badly and is not polite.

It is rude to stare at people.

◆ The opposite of rude is polite.

ruin *noun* (ruins)

A ruin is a building that is almost completely destroyed.

ruin *verb* (ruins, ruining, ruined)

If you ruin something, you spoil it completely.

rule *verb* (rules, ruling, ruled)

Someone who rules is in charge of a country and the people who live there.

rule *noun* (rules)

Rules tell you what you can and cannot do. Games have rules, and places like schools have rules too.

ruler *noun* (rulers)

1 A ruler is a strip of wood or plastic used for measuring and drawing straight lines.

2 A ruler is also someone who rules a country.

run *verb* (runs, running, ran, run)

When you run, you use your legs to move quickly.

◆ Some other words that end with the letters 'un' are: bun fun gun sun

rung SEE **ring** *verb*

Have you rung the doorbell yet?

a
b
c
d
e
f
g
h
i
j
k
l
m
n
o
p
q
r
s
t
u
v
w
x
y
z

Ss

sad *adjective* (sadder, saddest)

If you are sad, you feel unhappy.

Kate was sad to leave her old school.

◆ The opposite of sad is happy.

Some other words that end with the letters 'ad' are: bad dad glad had.

safe *adjective* (safer, safest)

If someone is safe, they are free from danger.

safe *noun* (safes)

A safe is a strong metal box where money or valuable things can be kept.

The cat felt safe up the tree.

said SEE **say**

Simon said he was sorry.

sail *noun* (sails)

A sail is a large piece of strong cloth joined to a boat. The wind blows into the sail and makes the boat move.

sail *verb* (sails, sailing, sailed)

To sail means to travel in a boat.

We sailed across the Atlantic.

◆ A person who works on a boat or ship is a sailor.

salad *noun* (salads)

Salad is a mixture of raw vegetables, usually eaten as part of a meal.

salt *noun*

Salt is a white powder you put on food to give it flavour.

same

If two things are the same, they are like each other in every way.

◆ Some other words that end with the letters 'ame' are: blame flame frame game name tame

sand *noun*

Sand is powder made up of tiny bits of rock. Sand covers deserts and the land next to the sea.

◆ Some other words that end with the letters 'and' are: band hand land stand

sandal *noun* (sandals)

A sandal is an open shoe with straps that go over your foot. People wear sandals in warm weather.

sandwich *noun* (sandwiches)

A sandwich is two slices of bread with another food between them.

◆ The word sandwich comes from the name of the Earl of Sandwich, who invented this kind of meal so that he didn't have to stop playing cards to eat.

sang SEE **sing**

The mermaid sang a strange and beautiful song.

sank SEE **sink**

There was a hole in the boat and it sank.

sari *noun* (saris)

A sari is a long piece of cloth which many Asian girls and women wear.

sat SEE **sit**

Grandpa sat in an armchair by the fire.

◆ Some other words that end with the letters 'at' are: bat cat flat hat mat pat rat that

satellite *noun* (satellites)

A satellite moves in space around a planet. The moon is a satellite of the earth. Machines can be satellites too. They move around the Earth and other planets sending out and collecting information.

◆ The word satellite comes from a Latin word that means 'a follower' or 'a guard'.

Little words can hide in big words. Can you see the words sat, at, ate, tell, and it hiding in the word satellite?

Saturday *noun* (Saturdays)

Saturday is the seventh day of the week.

a b c d e f g h i j k l m n o p q r **s** t u v w x y z

133

a
b
c
d
e
f
g
h
i
j
k
l
m
n
o
p
q
r
s
t
u
v
w
x
y
z

saucepan *noun* (saucepans)

A saucepan is made of metal. It has a lid and a long handle. Saucepans are used to cook food.

saucer *noun* (saucers)

A saucer is a small plate for putting a cup on.

sausage *noun* (sausages)

A sausage is made of tiny pieces of meat mixed with herbs and put into a thin skin.

save *verb* (saves, saving, saved)

1 If you save something, you keep it so that you can use it later.

I'm saving money for a new football shirt.

2 To save also means to keep someone or something safe from danger.

A helicopter saved two men whose boat had sunk.

saw *noun* (saws)

A saw is a tool that has a blade with sharp teeth on one edge. Saws are used for cutting material like wood.

saw SEE **see**

I saw you taking another chocolate from the box.

◆ The word saw sounds just like sore.

say *verb* (says, saying, said)

When you say something, you use your voice to make words.

She was too nervous to say her name.

◆ Some other words that end with the letters 'ay' are: day hay lay may pay play ray stay way

scale *noun* (scales)

A scale is one of the small, thin pieces of hard skin that cover fish and reptiles.

scales *noun*

Scales are used to find out how heavy things are.

scared *adjective*

Someone who is scared feels afraid.

Little Miss Muffet is scared of spiders.

◆ Other words that mean the same as scared are afraid and frightened.

school *noun* (schools)

School is the place where children go to learn.

science *noun* (sciences)

Science is finding out about things that happen in the world around us. We do this by measuring things and by doing tests called experiments.

scissors *noun*

A pair of scissors is a tool for cutting paper or cloth. It has two sharp blades joined in the middle.

score *verb* (scores, scoring, scored)

To score means to get a goal or a point in a game.

score *noun* (scores)

The score is the number of points or goals each side has in a game.

scratch *verb* (scratches, scratching, scratched)

1 If you scratch something, you damage it by moving something sharp over it.
Be careful you don't scratch the table with those scissors.

2 To scratch also means to move fingernails or claws over skin.
That cat has just scratched me!

scream *verb* (screams, screaming, screamed)

If you scream, you cry out loudly, often because you are hurt or afraid.

screen *noun* (screens)

A screen is a smooth surface on which films or television programmes are shown. Computers have screens too.

sea *noun* (seas)

The sea is the salt water that covers most of the Earth's surface.

◆ The word *sea* sounds just like *see*.

seal *noun* (seals)

A seal is a furry animal that lives in the sea and on land. Seals have flippers for swimming.

search *verb* (searches, searching, searched)

When you search, you look very carefully for something.
I've searched everywhere for my watch but I can't find it.

seaside *noun*

The seaside is a place beside the sea where people go for a holiday.

season *noun* (seasons)

A season is one of the four parts of the year. The four seasons are called spring, summer, autumn, and winter.

seat *noun* (seats)

A seat is anything that people sit on.
Look, I've saved you a seat.

◆ Some other words that end with the letters 'eat' are: beat eat heat meat neat wheat

second

If something is second, it is the next one after the first.
The second letter of the alphabet is B.

secret *noun* (secrets)

A secret is something that you do not want other people to know about.
Can you keep a secret?

a b c d e f g h i j k l m n o p q r **s** t u v w x y z

a b c d e f g h i j k l m n o p q r **s** t u v w x y z

see *verb* (sees, seeing, saw, seen)

When you see, you use your eyes to get to know something.

Can you see the balloon in the sky?

◆ The word see sounds just like sea.

seed *noun* (seeds)

A seed is a tiny part of the fruit of a plant. When a seed is put in the ground, it can grow into a new plant.

seek *verb* (seeks, seeking, sought)

If you seek something, you try to find it.

They played 'hide and seek' all over the house.

seem *verb* (seems, seeming, seemed)

To seem means to appear or look a certain way.

You seem a bit quiet today.

seen SEE **see**

Have you seen my hamster anywhere?

sell *verb* (sells, selling, sold)

If someone sells you something, they let you have it for an amount of money.

Do you sell marbles?

◆ The opposite of sell is buy.

◆ Some other words that end with the letters 'ell' are: bell fell shell spell tell well yell

send *verb* (sends, sending, sent)

If you send a person or thing, you make them go somewhere.

I'm sending a card to Grandpa.

sensible *adjective*

Sensible people are good at knowing what is best to do.

It is sensible to wear warm clothes when it snows.

sent SEE **send**

Little Red Riding Hood's mother sent her to her grandmother's house.

serve *verb* (serves, serving, served)

If someone serves you in a place like a shop or restaurant, they help you get what it is you want.

Is anyone serving you?

set *noun* (sets)

A set is a group of things that belong together.

Salik got a magic set for his birthday.

set *verb* (sets, setting, set)

1 When something sets, it becomes solid or hard.

This jelly hasn't set yet.

2 When you set something somewhere, you put it down.

Jenny set the plates on the table.

settee *noun* (settees)

A settee is a long comfortable seat with a back, for more than one person.

seven *noun* (sevens)

Seven is the number 7.

As I was going to St Ives, I met a man with seven wives.

sew *verb* (sews, sewing, sewed, sewn)

To sew means to use a needle and thread to join pieces of cloth together, or to fix things on to cloth.

sewn SEE **sew**

I've just sewn a badge on to my jacket.

sex *noun* (sexes)

The sexes are the two groups that all people and animals belong to. One group is male and the other is female.

shadow *noun* (shadows)

A shadow is the dark shape that is made by something blocking out the light.

Your shadow gets longer as the sun goes down.

shake *verb* (shakes, shaking, shook, shaken)

1 When a thing shakes, it moves quickly up and down or from side to side.

The whole house shakes whenever a train goes past.

2 If you shake something, you make it shake.

Shake the bottle before you pour the ketchup.

shallow *adjective* (shallower, shallowest)

Something like water that is shallow is not deep.

I can stand up in the shallow end of the swimming pool.

◆ The opposite of shallow is deep.

Little words can hide in big words. Can you see the words shall, hall, all, allow, and low hiding in the word shallow?

shape *noun* (shapes)

The shape of something is the pattern that its outside edges make. Circles, squares, and triangles are all shapes.

Mum made me a cake in the shape of a train.

◆ Some other words that end with the letters 'ape' are: ape grape tape

share *verb* (shares, sharing, shared)

If you share something, you make it into parts and give them to other people.

We shared the cake among the four of us.

shark *noun* (sharks)

A shark is a large sea fish with lots of sharp teeth.

sharp *adjective* (sharper, sharpest)

Something sharp has an edge or point that can cut or make holes.

These scissors are sharp enough to cut cardboard.

◆ The opposite of sharp is blunt.

shave *verb* (shaves, shaving, shaved)

When people shave, they cut hair from their skin to make it smooth.

a
b
c
d
e
f
g
h
i
j
k
l
m
n
o
p
q
r
s
t
u
v
w
x
y
z

she

Maddie says she is bored.

shed *noun* (sheds)

A shed is a small wooden building. People often keep tools or bicycles in a shed.

sheep *noun* (sheep)

A sheep is an animal kept by farmers for its wool and meat.

◆ A female sheep is called a ewe. A male sheep is called a ram. A baby sheep is called a lamb.

Some other words that end with the letters 'eep' are: deep keep sleep steep

sheet *noun* (sheets)

1 A sheet is one of the large pieces of cloth that you put on a bed.

2 A sheet is also a flat piece of paper or glass.

◆ Some other words that end with the letters 'eet' are: feet greet meet street sweet

shelf *noun* (shelves)

A shelf is a long flat surface for putting things on. Bookcases and cupboards have shelves.

shell *noun* (shells)

A shell is the hard part on the outside of eggs, nuts, and some kinds of animals such as snails and tortoises.

◆ Some other words that end with the letters 'ell' are: bell fell sell spell tell well yell

shelter *noun* (shelters)

A shelter is a place that keeps people or animals out of the wind or rain.

There's a shelter at the bus stop.

shine *verb* (shines, shining, shone)

When something shines, it gives out light, or looks very bright.

The sun was shining and the sky was blue.

shiny *adjective* (shinier, shiniest)

When things are shiny, they look very bright.

I cleaned the windows to make them shiny.

ship *noun* (ships)

A ship is a large boat that takes people or things across the sea.

◆ Some other words that end with the letters 'ip' are: chip drip hip lip slip trip

shirt *noun* (shirts)

You wear a shirt on the top half of your body. Shirts have sleeves, a collar, and buttons down the front.

shiver *verb* (shivers, shivering, shivered)

When you shiver, you shake because you are cold or frightened.

shoe *noun* (shoes)

A shoe is a strong covering for your foot.

shone SEE **shine**

Aladdin rubbed the lamp until it shone.

shook SEE **shake**

I shook my money box, but there was nothing in it.

shop *noun* (shops)

A shop is a place where people go to buy things.

◆ Some other words that end with the letters 'op' are: chop drop hop stop top

short *adjective* (shorter, shortest)

1 A short distance or time is not very long.

It was a short walk to the shops.
We only have time for a short visit.

2 A short person is not very tall.

◆ The opposite of short is long or tall.

shorts *noun*

Shorts are short trousers that end above your knees.

should

You should wrap up warm when it's cold outside.

shoulder *noun* (shoulders)

Your shoulder is the part of your body between your neck and the top of your arm.

shout *verb* (shouts, shouting, shouted)

When you shout, you speak very loudly.

Isabel shouted for help from the top of the tree.

show *verb* (shows, showing, showed, shown)

1 When you show something, you let someone else see it.

Show me the picture you've done.

2 If someone shows you how to do something, they do it so that you can watch them and learn how to do it.

Can you show me how to make a paper aeroplane?

show *noun* (shows)

A show is something that is put on for you to watch, like a television programme, a play, or dancing.

We are all going to a puppet show tonight.

shower *noun* (showers)

1 A shower is rain or snow that falls for only a short time.

Dr Foster went to Gloucester in a shower of rain.

2 A shower in the bathroom gives you a spray of water so that you can stand under it and wash all over.

◆ Little words can hide in big words. Can you *see* the words show, how, owe, and we hiding in the word shower?

shown SEE **show** *verb*

Have you shown Dan your hamsters?
Dad's shown me how to ride a bike.

a b c d e f g h i j k l m n o p q r **s** t u v w x y z

shut *verb* (shuts, shutting, shut)

To shut means to move a cover, lid, or door to block up an opening.

Please shut the door behind you.

◆ Another word that means the same as shut is close.

The opposite of shut is open.

shy *adjective* (shyer, shyest)

Someone who is shy is a bit nervous about talking to people they don't know.

sick *adjective* (sicker, sickest)

Someone who is sick does not feel well.

◆ Some other words that end with the letters 'ick' are: brick chick click flick kick lick pick quick stick thick trick

140

side *noun* (sides)

1 The side is the part that is on the left or right of something.

You start reading on the left side of the page.

2 A side can be an edge.

A triangle has three sides.

3 A side can also be a flat surface.

A cube has six sides.

4 The two sides in a game are the groups playing against each other.

◆ Some other words that end with the letters 'ide' are: bride hide pride ride tide wide

sign *noun* (signs)

A sign is anything that is written, drawn, or done to tell or show people something.

Did you see the sign for the nature park?

sign *verb* (signs, signing, signed)

When you sign something, you write your name.

We can all sign Emma's birthday card.

silent *adjective*

A person or thing that is silent does not make any sound at all.

Everyone was silent when the king started to speak.

◆ If you mix up all the letters in the word silent, you can make the word listen.

silk *noun*

Silk is a very fine, shiny material. It is made from threads spun by an insect called a silkworm.

silly *adjective* (sillier, silliest)

A silly person does something that is funny or not sensible.

It was silly of you to go out with such a bad cold.

silver *noun*

Silver is a valuable, shiny white metal.

sing *verb* (sings, singing, sang, sung)

When you sing, you make music with your voice.

◆ Some other words that end with the letters 'ing' are: bring king ring sting string swing thing wing

sink *noun* (sinks)

A sink is a place where you can wash things.

sink *verb* (sinks, sinking, sank, sunk)

If something sinks, it goes downwards, usually under water.

◆ The opposite of sink is float.

sister *noun* (sisters)

Your sister is a girl who has the same parents as you do.

sit *verb* (sits, sitting, sat)

When you sit, you rest on your bottom on a chair or on the floor.

six *noun* (sixes)

Six is the number 6.

size *noun* (sizes)

The size of something is how big it is.

Baby Bear's chair was the right size.

a b c d e f g h i j k l m n o p q r **s** t u v w x y z

a
b
c
d
e
f
g
h
i
j
k
l
m
n
o
p
q
r
s
t
u
v
w
x
y
z

skate *noun* (skates)

An ice skate is a special boot with a steel blade fixed underneath. A roller skate has small wheels instead of a blade.

skeleton *noun* (skeletons)

A skeleton is all the bones that hold up the body of a person or animal.

◆ Why didn't the skeleton go to the party?
Beccause he had no body to go with.

skin *noun* (skins)

1 Your skin is the outer covering of your body.

2 The outer covering of fruit and vegetables is also called skin.

skirt *noun* (skirts)

A skirt is worn by women and girls. It hangs down from the waist.

sky *noun* (skies)

The sky is the space above the Earth where you can see the clouds, sun, moon, and stars.

sleep *verb* (sleeps, sleeping, slept)

When you sleep, you close your eyes and let your body rest as it does every night.

◆ Some other words that end with the letters 'eep' are: deep keep sheep steep

sleeve *noun* (sleeves)

A sleeve is the part of something like a coat or shirt that covers your arm.

These sleeves are much too long.

slept SEE **sleep**

Sleeping Beauty slept for a hundred years.

slice *noun* (slices)

A slice of something like bread or cake is a thin piece cut from the whole thing.

slide *verb* (slides, sliding, slid)

If you slide, you move smoothly over something slippery or polished.

slide *noun* (slides)

A slide is a smooth slope that you can slide down for fun.

slip *verb* (slips, slipping, slipped)

If you slip, you slide suddenly without meaning to.

◆ Some other words that end with the letters 'ip' are: chip drip hip lip ship trip

slipper *noun* (slippers)

A slipper is a soft shoe that people wear indoors.

slippery *adjective*

Something slippery is so wet that it is difficult to get hold of or walk on.
Be careful, the pavement is slippery.

slope *noun* (slopes)

A slope is ground that is like the side of a hill, with one end lower than the other.
The ball rolled away down the slope.

slow *adjective* (slower, slowest)

Someone or something that is slow does not move very fast or takes a long time.

◆ If you take a long time to do something, you do it slowly.

The opposite of slow is fast or quick.

slug *noun* (slugs)

A slug is a small, slimy animal like a snail without its shell.

small *adjective* (smaller, smallest)

Small things are not as big as others of the same kind.
Mice are small animals.

◆ The opposite of small is big or large.

smash *verb* (smashes, smashing, smashed)

If something smashes, it breaks into lots of pieces with a loud noise.

143

a
b
c
d
e
f
g
h
i
j
k
l
m
n
o
p
q
r
s
t
u
v
w
x
y
z

a
b
c
d
e
f
g
h
i
j
k
l
m
n
o
p
q
r
s
t
u
v
w
x
y
z

smell *verb* (smells, smelling, smelt or smelled)

1 When you smell something, you use your nose to find out about it.

I can smell something burning.

2 When something smells, you can find out about it with your nose.

That rose smells nice.

smile *verb* (smiles, smiling, smiled)

When you smile, your face shows that you are feeling happy.

◆ What's the longest word in the dictionary? 'Smiles' because there's a mile between the first letter and the last.

smoke *noun*

Smoke is a grey or black cloud of gas that floats up from a fire.

smooth *adjective* (smoother, smoothest)

Something that is smooth does not have any lumps or rough parts.

The baby's skin is very smooth.

◆ The opposite of smooth is rough.

snail *noun* (snails)

A snail is a small, soft creature that lives inside a shell. Snails move very slowly.

snake *noun* (snakes)

A snake is a reptile with a long body and no legs. Some snakes can give poisonous bites.

sneeze *verb* (sneezes, sneezing, sneezed)

When you sneeze, you make a sudden noise as air rushes out of your nose.

I must have a cold — I can't stop sneezing.

snow *noun*

Snow is small, white pieces of frozen water. It floats down from the sky when the weather is very cold.

snowman *noun* (snowmen)

A snowman is a shape of a person made out of snow.

so

I am so tired I could sleep on the floor.

soap *noun*

You use soap with water for washing. Soap can be solid, liquid, or a powder.

sock *noun* (socks)

A sock is a soft covering for your foot and part of your leg.

soft *adjective* (softer, softest)

Something that is soft is not hard or firm.

The princess loved her soft bed.

◆ The opposite of soft is hard.

soil *noun*

Soil is the earth that plants grow in.

sold SEE **sell**

Amy sold Tom her recorder.

◆ Some other words that end with the letters 'old' are: bold cold fold gold hold old told

soldier *noun* (soldiers)

A soldier is a person in an army.

solid *adjective*

1 Something that is solid does not have space inside.

This is a solid chocolate egg.

2 Something that is solid does not easily change its shape. Liquids and gases are not solid, but rocks and metals are.

◆ The opposite of the first meaning of solid is hollow.

some

There are some roses growing in the garden.

◆ The word some sounds just like sum.

something

I thought I heard something moving outside the tent.

◆ Little words can hide in big words. Can you see the words so, some, me, met, thin, thing, and in hiding in the word something?

sometimes

Sometimes I go to school by bus.

son *noun* (sons)

A person's son is their male child.

Daddy is Grandpa's son.

◆ The word son sounds just like sun.

song *noun* (songs)

A song is words that are sung.

soon

Soon means in a short time.

I'll see you soon.

sore *adjective* (sorer, sorest)

Something that is sore feels painful.

I've got a sore throat and it hurts when I talk.

◆ The word sore sounds just like saw.

sorry

You say you are sorry when you have done something wrong.

I'm sorry I forgot your birthday.

sort *noun* (sorts)

If things are of the same sort, they belong to the same group or kind.

What sort of cake would you like?

sort *verb* (sorts, sorting, sorted)

When you sort things, you arrange them into different groups.

sound *noun* (sounds)

A sound is anything you can hear.

I heard the sound of a dog barking.

soup *noun*

Soup is a liquid food made from vegetables or meat and water. You eat soup with a spoon out of a bowl.

sour *adjective*

1 Things that are sour have the kind of taste a lemon or vinegar has.

2 If milk is sour, it is not fresh.

◆ The opposite of sour is sweet.

south *noun*

South is a direction. If you look towards the place where the sun comes up in the morning, south is on your right.

a
b
c
d
e
f
g
h
i
j
k
l
m
n
o
p
q
r
s
t
u
v
w
x
y
z

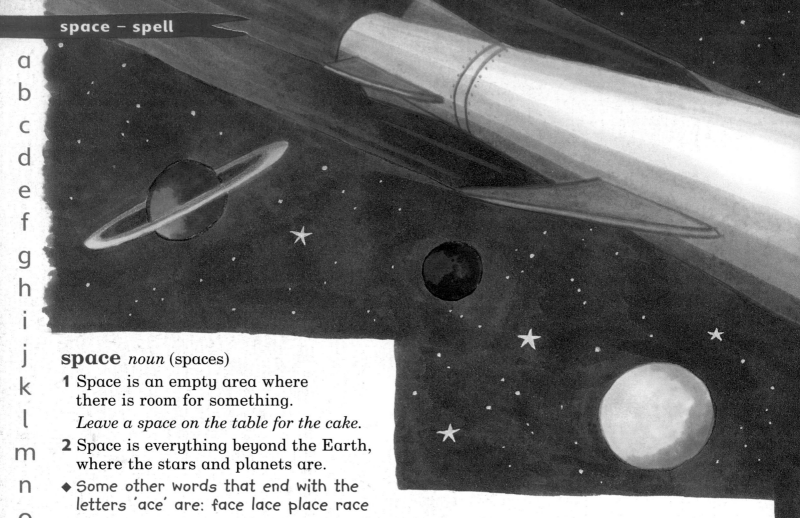

a b c d e f g h i j k l m n o p q r **s** t u v w x y z

space *noun* (spaces)

1 Space is an empty area where there is room for something.

Leave a space on the table for the cake.

2 Space is everything beyond the Earth, where the stars and planets are.

◆ Some other words that end with the letters 'ace' are: face lace place race

spaceship *noun* (spaceships)

A spaceship is a vehicle that can carry people and things through space.

spade *noun* (spades)

A spade is a tool used for digging. It has a long handle and a short, wide blade.

speak *verb* (speaks, speaking, spoke, spoken)

If you speak, you say something.

special *adjective*

1 If something is special, it is better than the usual kind.

Mum made a special cake for the party.

2 Special also means made for a particular job.

You need special shoes for tap dancing.

speed *noun* (speeds)

Speed is how quickly something moves or happens.

The car raced past at great speed.

spell *verb* (spells, spelling, spelt or spelled)

When you spell a word, you say or write the letters in the right order.

H o r s e spells horse.

spell *noun* (spells)

In stories, a spell is words that make magic things happen.

The wizard said a spell that turned his cat into a mouse.

◆ Some other words that end with the letters 'ell' are: bell fell sell shell tell well yell

spend *verb* (spends, spending, spent)

1 When you spend money, you use it to pay for things.

2 When you spend time, you use it to do something.

I'd like to spend an hour writing some letters to my friends.

spent SEE **spend**

I've spent all my pocket money on sweets.

We spent the weekend painting my room.

spider *noun* (spiders)

A spider is a small creature with eight legs. Many spiders make webs to catch insects to eat.

◆ The word spider comes from an old word that means 'a spinner'.

147

a b c d e f g h i j k l m n o p q r **s** t u v w x y z

spill *verb* (spills, spilling, spilt or spilled)

If you spill a liquid, you let it flow out when you do not mean to.

spin *verb* (spins, spinning, spun)

1 To spin means to turn round and round quickly.

The coin kept spinning on the table.

2 To spin also means to make thread by twisting long, thin pieces of wool or cotton together.

◆ Some other words that end with the letters 'in' are: bin chin pin thin tin twin win

spine *noun* (spines)

1 Your spine is the long row of bones down the middle of your back.

2 Spines are prickles or thorns on an animal or plant.

spire *noun* (spires)

A spire is a tall, pointed part of a church.

The church spire is so high you can see it for miles.

spiteful *adjective*

Someone who is spiteful says or does nasty things to upset people.

splash *verb* (splashes, splashing, splashed)

When liquid splashes, it flies about in drops.

The water splashed all over me.

spoil *verb* (spoils, spoiling, spoilt or spoiled)

If something is spoilt, it is not as good as it was before.

The rain spoilt my new shoes.

spoke SEE **speak**

The old man spoke very softly.

spoken SEE **speak**

Have you spoken to your new neighbours yet?

spoon *noun* (spoons)

You use a spoon to eat things like soup, cereal, and ice cream.

sport *noun* (sports)

A sport is a game that you play to get exercise and have fun. Football, tennis, and swimming are sports.

spot *noun* (spots)

1 A spot is a round mark.

A leopard's coat has dark spots.

2 A spot is also a small, red bump on your skin.

3 A spot can mean a place.

Here's a good spot for a picnic.

spout *noun* (spouts)

A spout is part of something like a teapot, kettle, or jug. It is made so that you can pour liquid out easily.

spring *noun* (springs)

1 Spring is the part of the year when plants start to grow and the days get longer and warmer.

2 A spring is a piece of metal that is wound into rings. It jumps back into shape after you press it down or stretch it.

◆ Spring is between winter and summer.

spun SEE **spin**

I spun round until I was dizzy.

square *noun* (squares)

A square is a shape with four corners and four sides that are the same length.

squirrel *noun* (squirrels)

A squirrel is a small wild animal with a long, bushy tail. Squirrels live in trees and eat nuts.

stable *noun* (stables)

A stable is a building where horses are kept.

stair *noun* (stairs)

A stair is one of a set of steps for going up or down inside a building.

Matthew went up the stairs to bed.

◆ Some other words that end with the letters 'air' are: air chair fair hair pair

stamp *noun* (stamps)

A stamp is a small piece of paper that you stick on an envelope or parcel before you post it.

stand *verb* (stands, standing, stood)

When you stand, you are on your feet without moving.

Don't just stand there — give me a hand.

◆ Some other words that end with the letters 'and' are: band hand land sand

star *noun* (stars)

1 A star is one of the tiny, bright lights you see in the sky at night.

2 A star is also somebody famous, like a singer or actor.

◆ Some other words that end with the letters 'ar' are: bar car far jar

start *verb* (starts, starting, started)

When you start, you take the first steps in doing something.

My sister is just starting to read.

◆ Another word that means the same as start is begin.

The opposite of start is finish or end or stop.

station *noun* (stations)

1 A station is a place where people get on or off trains.

2 A station is also a building for the police or fire brigade.

stay *verb* (stays, staying, stayed)

1 If you stay somewhere, you do not move away from there.

Stay here — I'll be back in a minute.

2 If you stay with someone or stay at a hotel, you spend the night there.

◆ Some other words that end with the letters 'ay' are: day hay lay may pay play ray say way

steady *adjective* (steadier, steadiest)

Something that is steady is not shaking at all.

Hold the ladder steady while I climb up.

steal *verb* (steals, stealing, stole, stolen)

To steal is to take something that belongs to someone else.

◆ The word steal sounds just like steel.

a
b
c
d
e
f
g
h
i
j
k
l
m
n
o
p
q
r
s
t
u
v
w
x
y
z

steam *noun*

Steam is very hot water that has turned into a cloud.

steel *noun*

Steel is a strong metal made from iron.

◆ The word steel sounds just like steal.

steep *adjective* (steeper, steepest)

If a slope is steep, it is hard to climb.

◆ Some other words that end with the letters 'eep' are: deep keep sheep sleep

stem *noun* (stems)

1 A stem is the main part of a plant above the ground.

2 A stem can also be the thin part that holds a leaf, flower, or fruit on to the rest of the plant.

step *noun* (steps)

1 A step is the movement you make with your foot when you are walking, running, or dancing.

2 A step is also a flat place where you can put your foot when you are going up or down stairs or a ladder.

stick *noun* (sticks)

A stick is a long, thin piece of wood or something else.

stick *verb* (sticks, sticking, stuck)

1 If something sticks to something else, it becomes fixed to it.

The peanut butter is sticking to the roof of my mouth.

2 If you stick something sharp into a thing, you push the point in.

What happens when you stick a pin in a balloon?

◆ Some other words that end with the letters 'ick' are: brick chick click flick kick lick pick quick sick thick trick

stiff *adjective* (stiffer, stiffest)

Something that is stiff is not easy to bend.

I need some stiff cardboard to make a crown.

still

Still means not moving at all.

Sit still while I brush your hair.

◆ Some other words that end with the letters 'ill' are: bill fill hill ill kill pill till will

sting *noun* (stings)

A sting is a sharp point with poison on it that some animals and plants have.

sting *verb* (stings, stinging, stung)

If something stings you, it hurts you with its sting.

A bee can sting you.

◆ Some other words that end with the letters 'ing' are: bring king ring sing string swing thing wing

stir *verb* (stirring, stirred)

When you stir a liquid or a soft mixture, you move it around with a spoon or stick.

stole SEE **steal**

The thief stole the king's ring.

stolen SEE **steal**

'Someone has stolen my ring,' said the king.

stomach *noun* (stomachs)

Your stomach is the part of your body where your food goes after you swallow it.

stone *noun* (stones)

1 A stone is a small piece of rock.

2 A stone is also the hard seed in the middle of some fruits such as cherries and plums.

stood SEE **stand**

We stood at the bus stop for ages.

stop *verb* (stops, stopping, stopped)

1 If a person or thing stops doing something, they do not do it any more.

It stopped raining and the sun came out.

2 If something that is moving stops, it comes to rest.

The bus stopped to let the people off.

◆ Some other words that end with the letters 'op' are: chop drop hop shop top

store *verb* (stores, storing, stored)

If you store something, you keep it until it is needed.

storm *noun* (storms)

A storm is very bad weather with strong wind and a lot of rain. There is sometimes thunder and lightning too.

story *noun* (stories)

A story tells you about something that has happened. Stories can be made up, or they can be about real things.

a
b
c
d
e
f
g
h
i
j
k
l
m
n
o
p
q
r
s
t
u
v
w
x
y
z

straight *adjective* (straighter, straightest)

Something that is straight has no bends or curves in it.

We could see a long, straight road in front of us.

strange *adjective* (stranger, strangest)

If something is strange, it is not like anything you have seen or heard before.

What a strange creature you have drawn!

straw *noun* (straws)

1 Straw is the dry stems of corn and wheat.

2 A straw is a very thin tube for drinking through.

strawberry *noun* (strawberries)

A strawberry is a small, red fruit. It has tiny seeds on the outside.

stream *noun* (streams)

A stream is a small river.

street *noun* (streets)

A street is a road with houses and other buildings along each side.

◆ Some other words that end with the letters 'eet' are: feet greet meet sheet sweet

strength *noun*

Strength is how strong someone or something is.

stretch *verb* (stretches, stretching, stretched)

When you stretch something, you pull it to make it longer, wider, or tighter.

The skin on a drum is stretched tight.

strict *adjective* (stricter, strictest)

When someone is strict, they make people do what they say and obey the rules.

Our new teacher is very strict.

string *noun*

String is very thin rope.

◆ Some other words that end with the letters 'ing' are: bring king ring sing sting swing thing wing

strip *noun* (strips)

A strip is a long, thin piece of something.

A picture frame is made from strips of wood.

stripe *noun* (stripes)

A stripe is a thin band of colour.

Tigers have stripes on their bodies.

strong *adjective* (stronger, strongest)

1 Strong people or animals are healthy and can carry heavy things and work hard.

2 Something strong is hard to break or damage.

We tied the boat with a strong rope.

3 Food or drink that is strong has a lot of flavour.

These mints are strong.

◆ The opposite of strong is weak.

stuck SEE **stick** *verb*

Pooh's paw has stuck to the jar of honey.

Tim stuck a pin in my balloon and it went bang.

stung SEE **sting** *verb*

I've just been stung by a bee.

submarine *noun* (submarines)

A submarine is a ship that can travel under water as well as on the surface.

suck *verb* (sucks, sucking, sucked)

If you suck something, you draw liquid from it into your mouth.

sudden *adjective*

Things that are sudden happen quickly when you do not expect them.

There was a sudden crash of thunder.

suddenly

If something happens suddenly, it happens quickly without any warning.

Suddenly all the lights went out.

sugar *noun*

Sugar is used to put in foods and drinks to make them taste sweet.

sum *noun* (sums)

A sum is a problem that you work out using numbers.

◆ The word sum sounds just like some.

summer *noun* (summers)

Summer is the hottest season of the year.

◆ Summer is between spring and autumn.

sun *noun*

The sun gives the Earth heat and light. It is a star, and the Earth moves around it.

◆ Some other words that end with the letters 'un' are: bun fun gun run

Sunday *noun* (Sundays)

Sunday is the first day of the week.

sung SEE **sing**

I have not sung this song before.

sunk SEE **sink** *verb*

My boat has sunk to the bottom of the pond.

sunny *adjective* (sunnier, sunniest)

On a sunny day the sun is shining.

supermarket *noun* (supermarkets)

A supermarket is a big shop that sells food and other things. People help themselves to things as they go round, and pay for them on the way out.

supper *noun* (suppers)

Supper is a meal eaten in the evening.

Peter Rabbit went to bed without any supper.

a
b
c
d
e
f
g
h
i
j
k
l
m
n
o
p
q
r
s
t
u
v
w
x
y
z

sure *adjective* (surer, surest)

If you are sure about something, you believe it is true or right.

I am sure I locked the door.

surface *noun* (surfaces)

The surface is the outer or top part of something.

The table has a smooth and shiny surface.

surprise *noun* (surprises)

A surprise is something that you did not expect.

What a lovely surprise!

swallow *verb* (swallows, swallowing, swallowed)

When you swallow something, you make it go down your throat and into your stomach.

◆ Little words can hide in big words. Can you see the words wall, all, allow, and low hiding in the word swallow?

swam SEE **swim**

The dog jumped into the stream and swam to the other side.

swan *noun* (swans)

A swan is a large white bird with a long curved neck. Swans live by rivers and lakes.

◆ A young swan is called a cygnet.

sweep *verb* (sweeps, sweeping, swept)

When you sweep, you use a broom to clear away dust and litter.

sweet *adjective* (sweeter, sweetest)

Sweet things have the taste of sugar.

The opposite of sweet is sour.

◆ Some other words that end with the letters 'eet' are: feet greet meet sheet street

swept SEE **sweep**

Ben swept up all the leaves from the path.

swim *verb* (swims, swimming, swam, swum)

When you swim, you move your body through water using your arms and legs.

We like to swim in the stream when it's a hot day.

swing *verb* (swings, swinging, swung)

When something swings, it moves backwards and forwards from a fixed point.

It's fun to swing on a rope.

◆ Some other words that end with the letters 'ing' are: bring King ring sing sting string thing wing

switch *noun* (switches)

A switch is anything that you turn or press to start or stop something working.

sword *noun* (swords)

A sword is a long metal blade with a handle.

King Arthur had a magic sword called Excalibur.

swum SEE **swim**

Have you swum in the stream yet?

swung SEE **swing**

Mina swung across the stream on a rope.

syrup *noun*

Syrup is a sweet, thick liquid. Treacle is a kind of syrup.

◆ The word syrup comes from an Arabic word that means 'a drink'.

a
b
c
d
e
f
g
h
i
j
k
l
m
n
o
p
q
r
s
t
u
v
w
x
y
z

155

Tt

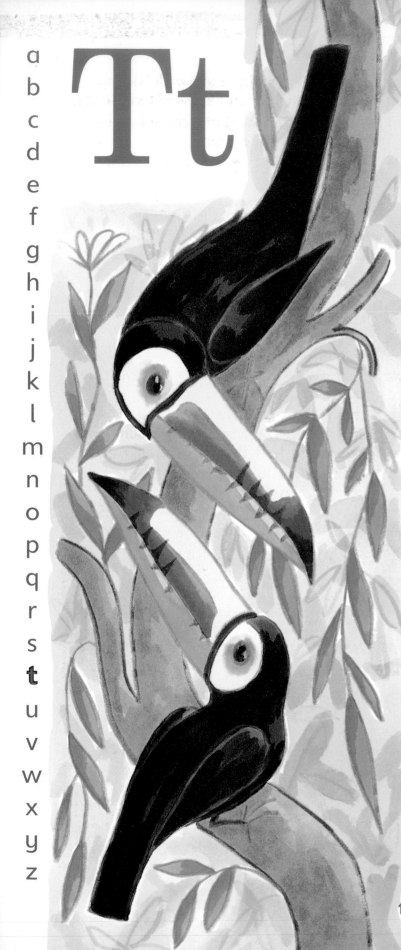

table *noun* (tables)

A table is a piece of furniture. It has legs and a flat top.

tadpole *noun* (tadpoles)

Tadpoles are the babies of frogs and toads. Tadpoles live in water.

tail *noun* (tails)

An animal's tail is the part that grows out from the back end of its body.

The puppy wagged its tail happily.

take *verb* (takes, taking, took, taken)

1 When you take something, you get it in your hands.

Please take my hand while we cross the road.

2 Take also means to bring or carry.

Don't forget to take your umbrella.

◆ Some other words that end with the letters 'ake' are: bake cake lake make

talk *verb* (talks, talking, talked)

When you talk, you speak to other people.

The wolf talked to Little Red Riding Hood in a squeaky voice.

tall *adjective* (taller, tallest)

A tall person or thing measures more than usual from top to bottom.

There's a very tall tree in our garden.

◆ The opposite of tall is short.

Some other words that end with the letters 'all' are: all ball call fall wall

tame *adjective* (tamer, tamest)

Tame animals are friendly to humans and not afraid of them.

◆ The opposite of tame is wild.

Some other words that end with the letters 'ame' are: blame flame frame game name same

tap *noun* (taps)

A tap lets you turn water on and off.

tape *noun* (tapes)

1 A tape is a special strip of plastic used to record sound or pictures.

2 Some tape has a sticky back. You can use it to hold paper together.

◆ Some other words that end with the letters 'ape' are: ape grape shape

taste *noun*

The taste of something is what it is like when you eat or drink it.

Monkeys love the taste of bananas.

taste *verb* (tasting, tasted)

When you taste something, you eat or drink a bit of it to see what it is like.

taught SEE **teach**

My brother has been taught to swim.

tea *noun* (teas)

1 Tea is a hot drink, made with boiling water and the dried leaves of tea plants.

2 Tea is also a meal that people have in the afternoon or evening.

◆ The word tea comes from a Chinese word.

teach *verb* (teaches, teaching, taught)

When someone teaches, they help people to understand something, or show them how to do it.

My aunt teaches people how to paint.

◆ The opposite of teach is learn.

teacher *noun* (teachers)

A teacher is someone whose job is to teach.

◆ Little words can hide in big words. Can you *see* the words tea, teach, each, ache, he, and her hiding in the word teacher?

a b c d e f g h i j k l m n o p q r s **t** u v w x y z

a
b
c
d
e
f
g
h
i
j
k
l
m
n
o
p
q
r
s
t
u
v
w
x
y
z

team *noun* (teams)

A team is a group of people who work together, or who play together on the same side.

Our team won last Saturday.

tear *noun* (tears)

A tear is a drop of water that falls from your eye when you cry.

◆ This word rhymes with here.

tear *verb* (tears, tearing, tore, torn)

If you tear something, you pull it apart.

Tear the paper along the dotted line.

◆ This word rhymes with hair.

teeth SEE **tooth**

telephone *noun* (telephones)

You use a telephone to speak to someone far away.

◆ The word telephone comes from two Greek words that mean 'far away' and 'sound'.

telescope *noun* (telescopes)

A telescope is a tube with lenses at both ends. It makes things that are far away look bigger and closer.

We looked at the stars through a telescope.

television *noun* (televisions)

A television is a machine that receives sounds and pictures through the air.

Johnny is watching television.

tell *verb* (tells, telling, told)

1 If somebody tells you something, they pass on news or information or a story.

The storyteller began to tell his tale.

2 If someone tells you to do something, they say you must do it.

Does your dog do what you tell it to do?

◆ Some other words that end with the letters 'ell' are: bell fell sell shell spell well yell

ten *noun* (tens)

Ten is the number 10.

tent *noun* (tents)

A tent is a shelter made of strong cloth stretched over poles. People live in tents when they are camping.

term *noun* (terms)

A term is part of a school year. It is the time in between the holidays, when the school is open.

test *noun* (tests)

A test is something you do to show how much you know.

than

A hare is bigger than a rabbit.

thank *verb* (thanks, thanking, thanked)

When you thank someone, you tell them you are grateful for something kind they have done.

Thank you for all my lovely presents.

that

Can I have that piece of cake, please?

◆ Some other words that end with the letters 'at' are:
bat cat flat hat mat pat rat sat

the

Look at the moon.

theatre *noun* (theatres)

A theatre is a place where you go to see plays and shows.

◆ The word theatre comes from a Greek word that means 'a place for seeing things'.

Little words can hide in big words. Can you see the words the, he, heat, eat, and at hiding in the word theatre?

their

The bees flew back to their hive.

them

Where are my gloves? I've lost them.

then

We had a picnic. Then we went to feed the ducks.

159

a
b
c
d
e
f
g
h
i
j
k
l
m
n
o
p
q
r
s
t
u
v
w
x
y
z

there

Do you want to sit here or there?

these

Do you like these pictures?

they

Look at these pictures. They are very good.

thick adjective (thicker, thickest)

1 Something that is thick measures a lot from one side to the other.

I'd like a thicker slice of cake.

2 Thick liquids do not flow easily.

I like thick honey.

◆ The opposite of thick is thin.

Some other words that end with the letters 'ick' are: brick chick click flick kick lick pick quick sick stick trick

thin adjective (thinner, thinnest)

1 A thin person or animal does not weigh very much.

2 Something that is thin does not measure much from one side to the other.

Thin paper tears easily.

◆ The opposite of the first meaning of thin is fat. The opposite of the second meaning of thin is thick.

Some other words that end with the letters 'in' are: bin chin pin spin tin twin win

think verb (thinks, thinking, thought)

When you think, you use your mind to work something out.

Can anyone think of the answer?

thirsty adjective (thirstier, thirstiest)

If you are thirsty, you need a drink.

Running makes me thirsty.

this

Do you want this cake or that one?

those

These flowers are nicer than those ones.

thought SEE think

I thought I saw a cat.

thread *noun* (threads)

A thread is a long, thin piece of something like cotton or wool.

three *noun* (threes)

Three is the number 3.

threw SEE throw

Raj threw a stone into the pond.

throat *noun* (throats)

Your throat is the front part of your neck, and the tubes inside that take food, drink, and air into your body.

◆ Some other words that end with the letters 'oat' are: boat coat float goat

through

Through means from one side or end to the other.
We crawled through a hole in the hedge.

throw *verb* (throws, throwing, threw, thrown)

When you throw something, you make it leave your hand and go through the air by moving your arm or hand.
'I'll throw these magic beans away!' thought Jack.

thrown SEE throw

I've thrown my ball over the wall.

thumb *noun* (thumbs)

Your thumb is the short, thick finger at the side of your hand.

thunder *noun*

Thunder is the loud noise that follows a flash of lightning in a storm.

thunderstorm *noun* (thunderstorms)

A thunderstorm is a storm with thunder and lightning.

Thursday *noun* (Thursdays)

Thursday is the fifth day of the week.

tidy *adjective* (tidier, tidiest)

If something is tidy, everything is in the right place and it is not in a mess.
Will keeps his room very tidy.

◆ A word that means the same as tidy is neat.

The opposite of tidy is messy or untidy.

tie *noun* (ties)

1 A tie is a long strip of material that is worn around the collar of a shirt and hangs down the front.
2 When two people do as well as each other in a race or have the same score in a game, it is called a tie.

tie *verb* (ties, tying, tied)

When you tie something, you make a knot.

a
b
c
d
e
f
g
h
i
j
k
l
m
n
o
p
q
r
s
t
u
v
w
x
y
z

a
b
c
d
e
f
g
h
i
j
k
l
m
n
o
p
q
r
s
t
u
v
w
x
y
z

tiger *noun* (tigers)

A tiger is a big wild cat found in India and China. It has orange fur with black stripes.

tight *adjective* (tighter, tightest)

If something is tight, it fits closely or is fastened firmly.

These shoes are too tight.

◆ The opposite of tight is loose.

Some other words that end with the letters 'ight' are: bright fight fright light night right

time *noun*

1 Time is measured in minutes, hours, days, and years.

2 The time is a particular moment in the day.

The White Rabbit kept looking at his watch to check the time.

tin *noun* (tins)

1 Tin is a silvery metal.

2 A tin is something that keeps food fresh.

◆ Some other words that end with the letters 'in' are: bin chin pin spin thin twin win

tiny *adjective* (tinier, tiniest)

Tiny things are very small.

tired *adjective*

When you are tired, you need to rest or sleep.

today

Today means on this day.

Today is my birthday.

toe *noun* (toes)

Your toe is one of the five parts at the end of your foot.

told SEE **tell**

We *told* each other ghost stories.

I *told* you to stop running around.

◆ Some other words that end with the letters 'old' are: bold cold fold gold hold old sold

tomorrow

Tomorrow means on the day after today.

See you tomorrow.

tongue *noun* (tongues)

Your tongue is the long, soft, pink part that you move inside your mouth.

tonight

Tonight means the night at the end of today.

We are going to watch the fireworks display tonight.

too

This coat is too small for me now.

◆ The word too sounds just like two.

took SEE **take**

I took a banana from the bowl.

It was lucky I took an umbrella.

◆ Some other words that end with the letters 'ook' are: book cook hook look

tool *noun* (tools)

A tool is something that you use in your hand to help you do a job. Hammers and saws are tools.

tooth *noun* (teeth)

A tooth is one of the hard, white parts in your mouth.

a b c d e f g h i j k l m n o p q r s **t** u v w x y z

163

top *noun* (tops)

1 The top of something is the highest part.
We climbed to the top of the hill.

2 The top is the part that covers something like a jar or tube.
Put the top back on your pen.

◆ The opposite of the first meaning of top is bottom.

Some other words that end with the letters 'op' are: chop drop hop shop stop

tore SEE **tear** *verb*
Yasmin tore out a sheet of paper.

toucan *noun* (toucans)
A toucan is a bird with a huge, brightly coloured beak and black and white feathers.

touch *verb* (touches, touching, touched)

1 If you touch something, you put your hand or fingers on it.

2 If things are touching, they are so close that there is no space between them.

towel *noun* (towels)
A towel is a piece of cloth to dry yourself with.

town *noun* (towns)
A town is a place with a lot of houses, shops, and other buildings.

◆ Some other words that end with the letters 'own' are: brown clown crown down frown

toy *noun* (toys)
A toy is something you play with.

tractor *noun* (tractors)
A tractor is a vehicle with a strong engine used for pulling heavy things on a farm.

traffic *noun*
Traffic is all the cars, buses, lorries, and other things travelling on the road.

train *noun* (trains)
A train carries people or things on railway lines.

train *verb* (trains, training, trained)
To train means to teach a person or animal how to do something.
I'm training my dog to walk on a lead.

◆ Some other words that end with the letters 'ain' are: brain chain drain grain main pain rain

travel *verb* (travels, travelling, travelled)
When you travel, you go on a journey.

tree *noun* (trees)
A tree is any tall plant with leaves, branches, and a thick stem of wood, called a trunk.
Let's play around this tree.

triangle *noun* (triangles)
A triangle is a shape with three straight sides and three points.

trousers *noun*
Trousers cover each leg and the lower part of your body.

truck *noun* (trucks)

1 A truck is a large vehicle that is used to carry things from place to place.

2 Trucks are also carts pulled by a railway engine. Trucks are used for carrying things like coal.

true *adjective* (truer, truest)

1 If a story is true, it really happened.

2 Something that is true is right.
Is it true that a whale is a mammal?

trunk *noun* (trunks)

1 A trunk is the thick, woody stem of a tree.

2 An elephant's trunk is its long nose.

3 A trunk is also a large box for storing things or carrying things on a journey.

try *verb* (tries, trying, tried)

If you try to do something, you see if you can do it.

Peter is trying to climb that tree.

tube *noun* (tubes)

1 Tubes are used to hold soft mixtures such as toothpaste.

2 A tube is also a kind of pipe.

Tuesday *noun* (Tuesdays)

Tuesday is the third day of the week.

tunnel *noun* (tunnels)

A tunnel is a long hole under the ground or through a hill.

The railway line goes through a tunnel.

turn *verb* (turns, turning, turned)

1 When you turn, you move round or change direction.

Please turn and face this way.

Turn left at the top of the hill.

2 When something turns into something else, it changes.

A caterpillar turns into a butterfly.

turn *noun* (turns)

If it is your turn, it is time for you to do something.

It's my turn to roll the dice.

tusk *noun* (tusks)

A tusk is one of the two long, pointed teeth that elephants have next to their trunk.

twelve *noun* (twelves)

Twelve is the number 12.

twin *noun* (twins)

Twins are two children who have the same parents and were born at the same time.

◆ Some other words that end with the letters 'in' are: bin chin pin spin thin tin win

twist *verb* (twists, twisting, twisted)

1 When you twist something, you turn or bend it.

My mum twisted her ankle running for a bus.

2 To twist also means to wrap things around each other.

Rope is made by twisting long threads together.

two *noun* (twos)

Two is the number 2.

◆ The word two sounds just like too.

tyre *noun* (tyres)

A tyre is a circle of rubber that goes round the edge of a wheel.

a b c d e f g h i j k l m n o p q r s **t** u v w x y z

Uu

ugly *adjective* (uglier, ugliest)

People and things that are ugly are not nice to look at.

Cinderella had two ugly sisters.

umbrella *noun* (umbrellas)

An umbrella is cloth stretched over a frame, which you hold over your head to keep off the rain.

◆ The word umbrella comes from an Italian word that means 'little shade', because umbrellas were first used to keep the sun off.

What goes up when the rain comes down? An umbrella.

uncle *noun* (uncles)

Your uncle is the brother of your mother or father, or the husband of your aunt.

under

Under means below.

Let's stand under a tree until it stops raining.

◆ The opposite of under is over.

understand *verb* (understands, understanding, understood)

If you understand something, you know what it means or how it works.

understood SEE **understand**

At last Harry understood how to do the puzzle.

undress *verb* (undresses, undressing, undressed)

When you undress, you take your clothes off.

unicorn *noun* (unicorns)

A unicorn is a creature in stories that looks like a white horse with a long horn in the middle of its forehead.

◆ The word unicorn comes from a Latin word that means 'one horn'.

uniform *noun* (uniforms)

A uniform is a special set of clothes people wear to show which school they go to or what job they do.

until

Until means up to a certain time.

You can stay until 4 o'clock.

up

Up means to a higher place.

The soldiers marched up the hill.

◆ The opposite of up is down.

upon

Upon means on top of.

The man had a green hat upon his head.

upright *adjective*

Something upright stands straight up.

A post stands upright in the ground.

upset *adjective*

When you are upset, you feel unhappy and sad.

upside down *adjective*

When something is upside down, the bottom part is at the top.

You're holding the picture upside down.

urgent *adjective*

Something urgent is very important and you need to act quickly.

This letter is urgent. It must go in the post tonight.

us

Thank you for inviting us.

use *verb* (uses, using, used)

When you use something, you do a job with it.

You'll have to use a screwdriver.

useful *adjective*

Something that is useful can be used to help you in some way.

usual *adjective*

Something that is usual is what happens most times.

We'll have dinner at the usual time.

a
b
c
d
e
f
g
h
i
j
k
l
m
n
o
p
q
r
s
t
u
v
w
x
y
z

Vv

valley *noun* (valleys)

A valley is the low land between hills or mountains.
The road runs through the valley.

valuable *adjective*

Valuable things are worth a lot of money.
This diamond ring is very valuable.

van *noun* (vans)

A van is a covered vehicle for carrying things and people.

◆ Some other words that end with the letters 'an' are: can gran man pan ran

vase *noun* (vases)

A vase is a pot for holding flowers.

vegetable *noun* (vegetables)

A vegetable is part of a plant that is used as food.

◆ There are many different types of vegetable. Here are some of them: aubergine, beans, cabbage, carrot, cauliflower, courgette, leek, marrow, onion, parsnip, peas, potato, pumpkin, spinach, yam

a b c d e f g h i j k l m n o p q r s t u **v** w x y z

village *noun* (villages)

A village is a group of houses together with other buildings in the country. A village is smaller than a town.

vehicle *noun* (vehicles)

A vehicle is anything that takes people and things from place to place. Cars, trucks, and bicycles are vehicles.

very

It is very cold in here.

vet *noun* (vets)

A vet is a person whose job is to take care of sick animals.

video *noun* (videos)

1 A video is sound and pictures recorded on special tape, to be shown on a television set.

2 A video is also a machine that can be used to play video tapes on a television set.

◆ The word video comes from a Latin word that means 'I see'.

visit *verb* (visits, visiting, visited)

When you visit someone, you go to see them.

◆ A person who visits a place is a visitor.

voice *noun* (voices)

Your voice is the sound you make when you are speaking or singing.

The big pirate had a very deep voice.

volcano *noun* (volcanoes)

A volcano is a mountain that sometimes has hot melted rock, gases, and ash bursting out of it.

◆ The word volcano comes from Vulcan, the name of the Roman god of fire.

What's the definition of a volcano? A mountain with a hiccup.

vulture *noun* (vultures)

A vulture is a large bird that eats dead animals.

Ww

wait *verb* (waits, waiting, waited)

If you wait, you stay for something that you are expecting to happen.

We stood waiting for the bus to come.

wake *verb* (wakes, waking, woke, woken)

When you wake up, you stop sleeping.

walk *verb* (walks, walking, walked)

When you walk, you move along by putting one foot in front of the other.

wall *noun* (walls)

1 A wall is any one of the sides of a building or room.

2 Walls made of brick or stone are also used round fields and gardens.

◆ Some other words that end with the letters 'all' are: all ball call fall tall

walrus *noun* (walruses)

A walrus is a large sea animal with two long tusks.

wand *noun* (wands)

A wand is a thin stick. In stories, fairies and wizards have wands. They use them for magic.

want *verb* (wants, wanting, wanted)

When you want something, you feel that you would like it.

What do you want for your birthday?

warm *adjective* (warmer, warmest)

If something is warm, it feels quite hot but not too hot.

◆ The opposite of warm is cool.

warn *verb* (warns, warning, warned)

If you warn someone, you tell them that there is danger.

Their mother warned the children not to go into the woods.

was

It was sunny yesterday.

wash *verb* (washes, washing, washed)

When you wash, you make something clean with water and soap.

Josh needs to wash his face.

wasp *noun* (wasps)

A wasp is a flying insect with black and yellow stripes. It has a sting.

waste *verb* (wastes, wasting, wasted)

If you waste something, you use more of it than you need.

She wastes water by leaving the tap running.

waste *noun*

Waste is things that are to be thrown away, usually because the useful part has been removed.

Put tins, rubbish, and other waste in the dustbin.

watch *verb* (watches, watching, watched)

If you watch something, you look to see what happens.

Claire and Will are watching cartoons.

watch *noun* (watches)

A watch is a small clock that you wear on your wrist.

water *noun*

Water is the liquid in rivers and seas. It falls from the sky as rain.

Josh will need plenty of water to get clean.

wave *verb* (waves, waving, waved)

If you wave, you move your hand about in the air.

We all waved goodbye as Auntie Alison drove off.

wave *noun* (waves)

A wave is a moving line of water on the surface of the sea.

The waves were crashing on to the beach.

wax *noun*

Wax is used to make candles, crayons, and polish. It is soft and melts easily. Some wax is made by bees, and some is made from oil.

way *noun* (ways)

1 The way to a place is how to get there.
Kirsty doesn't know which way to go.

2 The way to do something is how to do it.
This is the way to hold a baseball bat.

◆ The word way sounds just like weigh.

Some other words that end with the letters 'ay' are: day hay lay may pay play ray say stay

we

We live in a yellow house.

a b c d e f g h i j k l m n o p q r s t u v **w** x y z

171

a b c d e f g h i j k l m n o p q r s t u v **w** x y z

weak *adjective* (weaker, weakest)

People or things that are weak are not strong.

She felt so weak that she could not stand up.

◆ The opposite of weak is strong.

The word weak sounds just like week.

wear *verb* (wears, wearing, wore, worn)

1 When you wear something, you are dressed in it.

She was wearing a colourful jacket and a bright red hat.

2 If something wears out, it becomes weak and useless because it has been used too much.

◆ The word wear sounds just like where.

weather *noun*

The weather is how it is outside, for example sunny or raining.

◆ Little words can hide in big words. Can you see the words we, eat, at, the, and her hiding in the word weather?

web *noun* (webs)

A web is the same as a cobweb.

Wednesday *noun* (Wednesdays)

Wednesday is the fourth day of the week.

weed *noun* (weeds)

A weed is a plant that is growing where you do not want it.

week *noun* (weeks)

A week is seven days. There are 52 weeks in a year.

◆ The word week sounds just like weak.

a b c d e f g h i j k l m n o p q r s t u v **w** x y z

well

1 *adjective* (better, best)
If you are well, you are healthy.

◆ Some other words that end with the letters 'ell' are: bell fell sell shell tell yell

2 If you do something well, you are good at it, or make a good job of it.
You all played well today.

went SEE go

The owl and the pussycat went to sea.

were

The birds were singing this morning.

west *noun*

West is the direction you look in to see the sun go down in the evening.

wet *adjective* (wetter, wettest)

If something is wet, it is covered in water, or has water in it.

◆ The opposite of wet is dry.

whale *noun* (whales)

A whale is a very large sea animal. It breathes through a hole in the top of its head.

weigh *verb*
(weighs, weighing, weighed)

When you weigh something, you find out how heavy it is.

◆ The weight of something is how heavy it is.

The word weigh *sounds just like* way.

173

a
b
c
d
e
f
g
h
i
j
k
l
m
n
o
p
q
r
s
t
u
v
w
x
y
z

what

What do you want to drink?

wheat *noun*

Wheat is a plant grown by farmers. Its seed is used for making flour.

◆ Some other words that end with the letters 'eat' are: beat eat heat meat neat seat

wheel *noun* (wheels)

Wheels are round and they turn. Cars and bicycles move along on wheels.

wheelchair *noun* (wheelchairs)

A wheelchair is a chair that moves on wheels. It is used by people who cannot walk.

whisper *verb* (whispers, whispering, whispered)

When you whisper, you speak very softly.

'The giant is still asleep', whispered Jack.

whistle *verb* (whistles, whistling, whistled)

When you whistle, you make a loud, high sound by blowing air through your lips.

whistle *noun* (whistles)

A whistle is a small tube that makes a loud, high sound when you blow it.

white *adjective*

White is the colour of milk or snow.

◆ Some other words that end with the letters 'ite' are: bite kite write

when

When does the party start?

where

Where are all these birds going?

◆ The word where sounds just like wear.

which

Which bird do you like best?

◆ The word which sounds just like witch.

while

The giant snored while he was asleep.

who

Who is knocking at the door?

whole *adjective*

Whole means all of something, with nothing missing.

She read the whole book in one go.

◆ The word whole sounds just like hole.

why

Why did the chicken cross the road?

wide *adjective* (wider, widest)

Something that is wide measures a lot from side to side.

The stream is too wide to jump across.

◆ The opposite of wide is narrow.

Some other words that end with the letters 'ide' are: bride hide pride ride side tide

wild *adjective* (wilder, wildest)

Wild animals and plants live and grow without people looking after them.

◆ The opposite of wild is tame, when you are talking about animals.

will

I will see you later.

◆ Some other words that end with the letters 'ill' are: bill fill hill ill kill pill still till

win *verb* (wins, winning, won)

When you win, you beat everybody else in a game or race.

◆ The person who wins something is the winner.

The opposite of win is lose.

Some other words that end with the letters 'in' are: bin chin pin spin thin tin twin

wind *noun* (winds)

A wind is air moving along quickly.

The wind blew the leaves everywhere.

◆ When the wind is blowing hard, it is windy.

window *noun* (windows)

A window is an opening in the wall of a building, or in a vehicle. Windows are for letting in light and air. Most windows have glass in them.

◆ The word window comes from two Old Norse words that mean 'wind' and 'eye'.

wing *noun* (wings)

A wing is one of the parts of a bird or insect that it uses for flying. An aeroplane also has wings.

◆ Some other words that end with the letters 'ing' are: bring king ring sing sting string swing thing

winter *noun* (winters)

Winter is the coldest part of the year.

◆ Winter is between autumn and spring.

Why do birds fly south for the winter? It's too far to walk.

wire *noun* (wires)

A wire is a long strip of thin metal that can be bent easily.

wish *verb* (wishes, wishing, wished)

When you wish, you say or think what you would like to happen.

I wish I could have a puppy.

a b c d e f g h i j k l m n o p q r s t u v **w** x y z

witch *noun* (witches)

In stories, a witch is a woman who can do magic.

◆ The word witch sounds just like which.

with

Can I have a straw with my drink?

wizard *noun* (wizards)

In stories, a wizard is a man who can do magic.

We're off to see the wizard, the wonderful Wizard of Oz.

◆ The word wizard comes from an old word that means 'a wise person'.

woke SEE **wake**

Sleeping Beauty woke from a deep sleep.

woken SEE **wake**

She was woken by a kiss.

woman *noun* (women)

A woman is a fully grown female person.

won SEE **win**

I've won the game!

wood *noun* (woods)

1 Wood is the hard material that comes from trees. It can be used to make things like furniture and paper.

2 A wood is a lot of trees growing together.

◆ The word wood sounds just like would.

wool *noun*

Wool is the thick, soft hair that covers sheep. It is spun into thread and used for making cloth and for knitting.

word *noun* (words)

Words are what you use when you speak or write. Words that are written have a space on each side of them.

wore SEE **wear**

I wore my blue jumper yesterday.

work *noun*

Work is a job or something that you have to do.

world *noun* (worlds)

The world is the Earth and everything on it.

worm *noun* (worms)

A worm is a small animal with a long, thin body and no legs. Worms live in the ground.

worn SEE **wear**

My jeans are old and worn out.

worry *verb* (worries, worrying, worried)

When you worry, you keep thinking about something bad that might happen.

worse

Worse means not as good as.

Your singing is even worse than mine.

◆ The opposite of worse is better.

worst

Worst means so bad that none of the others are as bad as that.

Mildred Hubble is the worst witch in the world.

◆ The opposite of worst is best.

worth

If something is worth an amount of money, that is how much it could be sold for.

This old watch is worth a lot of money.

would

Would you like another piece of cake?

◆ The word would sounds just like wood.

wrap *verb* (wraps, wrapping, wrapped)

When you wrap something, you cover it in something like paper or cloth.

◆ When we say words that begin wr, we do not say the w. The letter w is silent.

wrist *noun* (wrists)

Your wrist is the thin part of your arm where it joins your hand.

write *verb* (writes, writing, wrote, written)

When you write, you put words on paper so that people can read them.

Faye is writing a letter to her uncle.

◆ A person who writes a book or story is called a writer or an author.

The word write sounds just like right.

Some other words that end with the letters 'ite' are: bite kite white

written SEE **write**

She has written lots of stories.

wrong *adjective*

Something that is wrong is not right.

You've got the last question wrong.

It is wrong to tell lies.

wrote SEE **write**

I wrote a letter to Grandma yesterday.

a b c d e f g h i j k l m n o p q r s t u v **w** x y z

Xx

X-ray *noun* (X-rays)

An X-ray is a special photograph that shows the inside of a body.

X-ray fish *noun* (X-ray fish)

An X-ray fish is a small fish with a body that you can see through.

xylophone *noun* (xylophones)

A xylophone is a musical instrument which you play by hitting the wooden or metal strips with small hammers.

Yy

yacht *noun* (yachts)

A yacht is a boat with sails.

yak *noun* (yaks)

A yak is a large animal with long hair and long horns.

yawn *verb* (yawns, yawning, yawned)

When you yawn, you open your mouth wide and take a deep breath. You yawn when you are tired or bored.

year *noun* (years)

A year is a measure of time. There are twelve months in a year.

yellow *adjective*

Yellow is the colour of lemons and butter.

Dorothy and her friends followed the yellow brick road.

yes

'Do you like bananas?' 'Yes, I do'.

yesterday

Yesterday means on the day before today.

It was my birthday yesterday.

a b c d e f g h i j k l m n o p q r s t u v w **x y** z

179

a
b
c
d
e
f
g
h
i
j
k
l
m
n
o
p
q
r
s
t
u
v
w
x
y
z

yogurt *noun* (yogurts)

Yogurt or yoghurt is a food made from milk. It tastes a little sour and often has fruit in it.

◆ The word yogurt comes from a Turkish word.

you

Happy Birthday to you!

young *adjective* (younger, youngest)

A person or animal that is young was born not long ago.

◆ The opposite of young is old.

your

Is this your pen?

180

Zz

zebra *noun* (zebras)

A zebra is an animal that looks like a horse with black and white stripes. Zebras live in Africa.

zigzag *noun* (zigzags)

A zigzag is a line which bends suddenly one way and then the other.

zip *noun* (zips)

A zip is used to fasten two edges of material together. Some dresses, trousers, and bags have zips.

zoo *noun* (zoos)

A zoo is a place where different kinds of wild animal are kept so that people can go and look at them.

181

the alphabet

Aa
anteater

Bb
bear

Cc
cow

Dd
donkey

Ee
elephant

Kk
kangaroo

Ll
lion

Mm
monkey

Nn
newt

Oo
owl

Uu
unicorn

Vv
vulture

Ww
walrus

Xx
X-ray fish

Yy
yak

Ff

fish

Gg
goat

Hh

hen

Ii

iguana

Jj

jaguar

Pp

panda

Qq
quetzal

Rr
rhino

Ss

snail

Tt
toucan

Zz
zebra

Grace   Mina   Katie   Robbie   Josh   Daniel

123 and counting

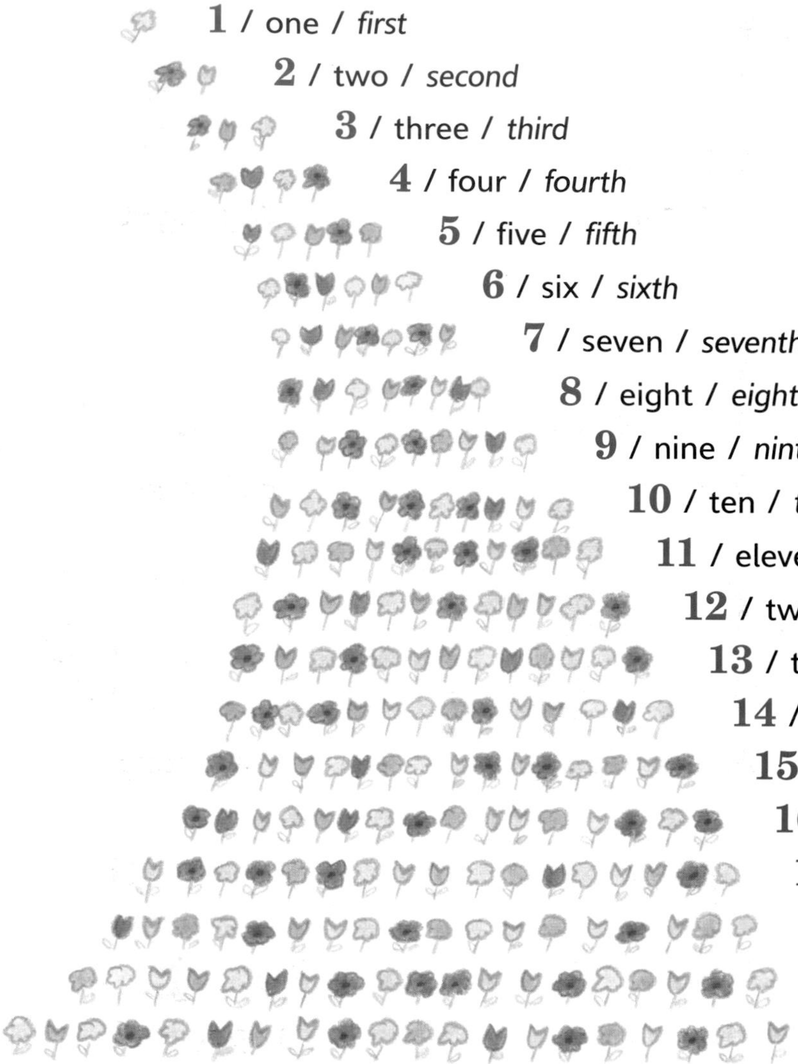

1 / one / *first*

2 / two / *second*

3 / three / *third*

4 / four / *fourth*

5 / five / *fifth*

6 / six / *sixth*

7 / seven / *seventh*

8 / eight / *eighth*

9 / nine / *ninth*

10 / ten / *tenth*

11 / eleven / *eleventh*

12 / twelve / *twelfth*

13 / thirteen / *thirteenth*

14 / fourteen / *fourteenth*

15 / fifteen / *fifteenth*

16 / sixteen / *sixteenth*

17 / seventeen / *seventeenth*

18 / eighteen / *eighteenth*

19 / nineteen / *nineteenth*

20 / twenty / *twentieth*

21 / twenty-one / *twenty-first*

30 / thirty / *thirtieth*

40 / forty / *fortieth*

50 / fifty / *fiftieth*

60 / sixty / *sixtieth*

70 / seventy / *seventieth*

80 / eighty / *eightieth*

90 / ninety / *ninetieth*

100 / a hundred / *hundredth*

Opposites

large small

fat thin

day night

old young

fast slow

soft hard

long short

inside outside

few many

wet dry

old new

happy sad

wide narrow

heavy light

open closed

dark light

high low

empty full

Colours and Shapes

pink

star

blue

triangle

red

square

green

circle

yellow

rectangle

grey

diamond

purple

semicircle

white

octagon

orange

oval

brown

pentagon

black

hexagon

Body words

finger

thumb

hair

ear

back

wing

fur

nose

beak

paw

knee

tail

foot

fin

trunk

eye

toe

head

heel

ankle

mouth

arm

leg

elbow

hand

tusk

shell

verbs (doing words)

build **call**
carry catch chase
clap climb crawl cry **cut**
dance dig drink eat **explore**
fall find **fly** frown grow hear
help hide **jump** **laugh** like listen
look make mix paint play **pull**
push **reach** run search **see** shout
sing **sit** sleep smell smile
splash **swim** talk **taste** throw
touch use walk **wash**
wrap yawn

Words we write a lot

a	call	end	her
about	called	every	here
after	came	everyone	hers
again	can		him
all	can't	first	his
am	cat	for	home
an	children	from	house
and	come		how
another	comes	get	
any	coming	getting	I
anyone	could	girl	if
are	cross	go	I'm
aren't		goes	in
as	dad	going	inside
at	day	gone	into
away	did	good	is
	didn't	got	isn't
	dig		it
back	do	had	its
ball	does	hadn't	it's (it is)
be	doesn't	half	
because	dog	has	jump
bed	doing	hasn't	just
been	done	have	
big	don't	haven't	last
boy	door	having	laugh
brother	down	he	like
but		help	liked
by			

little
live
lived
look
looked
lots
love

made
make
man
many
may
me
more
much
mum
must
my
myself

name
new
next
night
no
not
now

of
off
old
on
once
one
only
or
other
our
ours
out
outside
over

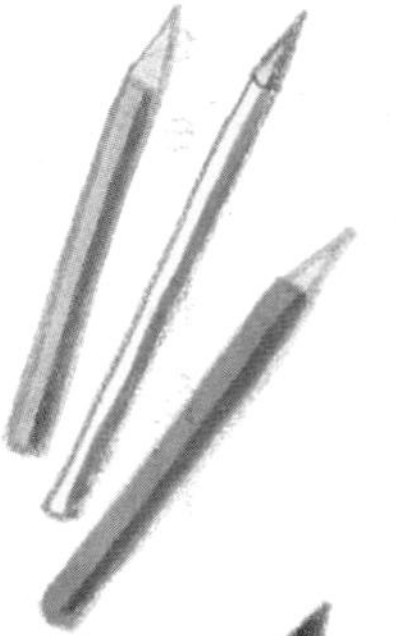

people
play
please
pull
pulled
push
put

ran

said
saw
school
see

seen
she
should
sister
sit
so
some

take
taken
than
thank
that
the
their
theirs
them
then
there
these
they
this
those
three
time
to
too
took
tree
two

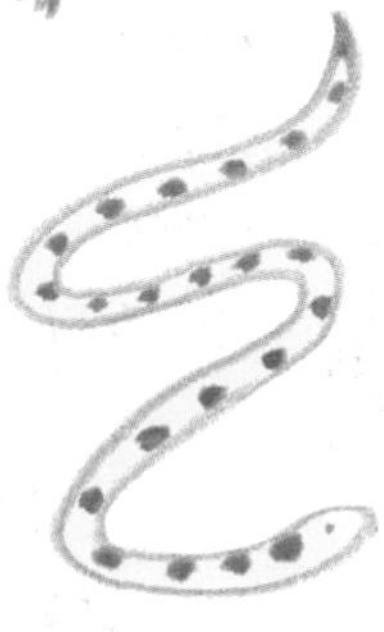

under
up
upon
us

very

want
was
wasn't
water
way
we
went
were
what
when
where
which
who
why
will
with
won't
would

yes
you
your
yours

Our world

mountain

cloud

forest

city

waterfall

lake

village

wood

bridge

stream

town

beach

bay

river

ship

coast

boat

cliff

field

island

lighthouse

waves

sea